翻译专业基础课系列教材

汉英翻译方法经典案例解析

主 编◎武光军 蒋雨衡

CHINESE-ENGLISH
TRANSLATION METHODS:
CASE ANALYSES

华东师范大学出版社
·上海·

图书在版编目（CIP）数据

汉英翻译方法经典案例解析 / 武光军，蒋雨衡主编.
上海 : 华东师范大学出版社，2024. -- ISBN 978-7
-5760-5125-4

Ⅰ. H315.9

中国国家版本馆CIP数据核字第2024LQ8280号

汉英翻译方法经典案例解析

主　　编　武光军　蒋雨衡
项目编辑　张　婧　袁一蒨
审读编辑　袁一蒨
责任校对　曹一凡　时东明
装帧设计　俞　越

出版发行　华东师范大学出版社
社　　址　上海市中山北路3663号　邮编 200062
网　　址　www.ecnupress.com.cn
电　　话　021-60821666　行政传真 021-62572105
客服电话　021-62865537　门市（邮购）电话 021-62869887
地　　址　上海市中山北路3663号华东师范大学校内先锋路口
网　　店　http://hdsdcbs.tmall.com

印 刷 者　浙江临安曙光印务有限公司
开　　本　787毫米×1092毫米　16开
印　　张　11
字　　数　235千字
版　　次　2024年9月第1版
印　　次　2024年9月第1次
书　　号　ISBN 978-7-5760-5125-4
定　　价　41.00元

出 版 人　王　焰

（如发现本版图书有印订质量问题,请寄回本社客服中心调换或电话021-62865537联系）

前　言

　　翻译方法是翻译学研究的重要课题,既有重要的理论意义,也有重要的实践意义。

　　首先,从理论意义方面来说,方梦之(2018:2)指出,翻译方法是翻译理论最原始、最基本的课题,意义能否转换、如何转换是古今中外翻译界长期讨论的问题。英国著名翻译理论家纽马克(Newmark,1988:19)甚至提出,翻译理论关注的主要问题就是为各类文本选择合适的翻译方法。翻译理论不是研究源语或目标语的语言机制,而是研究译者在翻译过程中为源语和目标语进行转换所需要开展的各种选择和决策(Newmark,1988:19)。刘宓庆(1999:162)认为,翻译方法论是翻译学中最重要的应用理论研究,其基本任务是探究双语转换的各种手段,阐明各种手段的基本作用机制理据,阐明方法论研究的理论原则和基本指导思想。

　　中外学者都在翻译方法研究方面做了大量的探索。在我国传统译学中,经常使用的术语是"翻译方法"或"翻译技巧",但后来又出现了"翻译策略"的提法。"翻译策略"一说于20世纪90年代中期开始出现在我国翻译研究中,差不多与"异化"同时引进(方梦之,2013:1)。翻译策略是指翻译过程中的思路、途径、方式和程序,是宏观理论桥接翻译实践的必由之路,贯穿于整个翻译过程。翻译策略既可由宏观理论推衍出来,也可由实践经验和技巧集约化、概念化、范畴化而得(方梦之,2013)。但国内外对翻译策略、翻译方法、翻译技巧的使用都存在模糊或混淆(熊兵,2014)。

　　为了更好地区分这三个概念,熊兵(2014)指出:翻译策略是翻译活动中,为实现特定翻译目的所依据的原则和所采纳的方案的集合;翻译方法是翻译活动中,基于某种翻译策略,为达到特定翻译目的所采取的特定的途径、步骤、手段;翻译技巧是翻译活动中,某种翻译方法在具体实施和运用时所需的技术、技能或技艺。这在一定程度上阐明了三个概念间的联系和区别。但在具体的分析中,又似乎很难落地。熊兵(2014)对三个概念的界定体系如下:首先,界定出两种翻译策略:异化与归化;然后,在异化策略下又析出了四种翻译方法,即零翻译、音译、逐词翻译和直译,在归化策略下也析出了四种翻译方法,即意译、仿译、改译和创译;最后,还归纳出了五种翻译技巧,即增译、减译、分译、合译及转换。对此,我们仍存在下列疑问:直译和意译仅是翻译方法,不是翻译策略吗? 增译、减译、分译、合译及转换这五种翻译技巧不是翻译方法吗? 或者说零翻译、音译、逐词翻译不是翻译技巧吗? 由此可见,当前翻译界还没有公认的用以区分这三个概念的方法或准则。因此,本书还是使用较为通用的"翻译方法"的概念。

国外学者对翻译方法进行了较为详细的探讨。纽马克(1988)共列出了16种翻译方法：转写(transcription)、一对一翻译(one-to-one translation)、借译(through-translation)、使用同义词(lexical synonymy)、成分分析(componential analysis)、转换词性(transposition)、转换视角(modulation)、补偿(compensation)、文化对等(cultural equivalence)、贴翻译标签(translation label)、下定义(definition)、扩展(expansion)、收缩(contraction)、句式重组(recasting sentences)、改良原文(rearrangement/improvement)、两法并用(translation couplet)。在范·多尔斯勒(van Doorslaer, 2009)的基础上，芒迪(Munday, 2010)列出了24种翻译方法：涵化(acculturation)、增译(amplification)、仿译(calque)、补偿(compensation)、浓缩(condensation)、转写(direct transfer)、扩展(expansion)、隐化(implicitation)、阐释(interpretation)、修改(modification)、再范畴化(recategorization)、添加(addition)、顺应(adaptation)、借用(borrowing)、造词(coinage)、简化(concision)、去名词化(denominalization)、淡化(dilution)、模仿(imitation)、互换(interchange)、转换视角(modulation)、释义(paraphrase)、重述(reformulation)和省略(omission)。

再者，从实践意义方面来说，翻译方法是我们开展翻译实践时须臾不可或缺的解决翻译问题或翻译难题的手段。由于汉语和英语之间存在较大差异，所以翻译实践中往往难以找到对应的翻译，就要对源语进行转换，这当然就意味着对翻译方法的科学运用。例如，在"扎实推进节能减排、生态建设和环境保护。"一句中，副词"扎实"就难以找到对应的英文词，就需运用翻译方法。一种较为合适的做法就是将该词转换为形容词"genuine"，译为"We made genuine progress in energy conservation, emissions reduction, ecological improvement and environmental protection."。

但我们发现学生们在使用这些具体的翻译方法时的苦恼是：一方面，不知何时该使用这些具体的翻译方法；另一方面，也不清楚这些具体的翻译方法之间的关系，特别是对于有些存在矛盾关系的翻译方法，如省略译法和增补译法。换言之，我们在具体翻译方法的层面尚未建立起系统性。我们认为，建立起具体翻译方法间系统性的路径，一是要阐述出这些方法的应用条件；二是要厘清这些方法间的对应关系。同时，我们认为特别要处理好成对的矛盾的翻译方法间的关系，要将这些成对的矛盾的翻译方法放在一起研究，研究它们的应用条件和对应关系。因此，本书精选了共五对、十种翻译方法：对应与转换、拆分与整合、虚化与实化、省略与增补以及移植与改写，详细探讨这些方法在汉译英实践中的应用条件和对应关系，以期通过探索汉译英中翻译方法论的系统性，加强学生对具体翻译方法的认识。

为生动形象地展现翻译方法在翻译实践中的运用，本书选取了大量我国现当代社会实践中产生的经典翻译案例,体裁多样,题材丰富,包括政治文本《习近平谈治国理政》、党的二十大报告,文学作品《边城》《家》,等等。本书结合翻译理论,对真实翻译案例进行解析,试图还原翻译过程,强调各翻译方法的应用条件,强化学生对这些方法的理解,并提高他们运用这些方法开展汉译英实践的能力。此外,每一章的末尾都提供了针对性的翻译练习。每套练习分为三个层次,分别是:译文补充、句子翻译与段落/诗歌翻译,难度逐级提升,旨在帮助学生自主检验学习成效,实实在在掌握汉英翻译方法,提高汉英翻译水平。

武光军

2024 年 5 月于北京

目　录

第一章

对应与转换

对应与转换是翻译方法中两个母体性的方法,即翻译中两种最基本的翻译方法。也就是说,其他翻译方法都是在这两种方法的基础上生成的。因此,对应与转换可以说是汉英翻译中两种基本的思维方式。

一、对应译法在汉译英中的应用

汉译英中的"对应"指的是概念上的对应或基本对应,即语义上所指的同一和语法上功能的基本相同(刘宓庆,2019:168-169)。刘宓庆(2019)指出了汉英对应的七种情况:

(1)人称代词及部分不定代词或指示代词;

(2)数词及其种种组合形式,各种数理公式、方程式;

(3)无多义或歧义的科学技术名词及专业术语;

(4)无多义或歧义的专名,包括人名、物名、地名、朝代名、年号名;

(5)无多义或歧义的名词、无歧义的定式搭配及常用的自由搭配,如太阳→sun、白雪→white snow、雨季→rainy season等;

(6)无变义或歧义的核心句,如我吃(SV)→I eat.、我爱音乐(SVO)→I love music.、他是加拿大人(SVC)→He's a Canadian.等;

(7)若干定式寒暄语,如再见→bye bye、早上好→good morning等。

这些情况下的对应是汉英翻译的基础。但实际上,在汉译英实践中,即使是代词和无多义或歧义的名词等也常常无法实现完全的对应,主要是部分的对应。

1.代词的对应

例1-1

中文原文

中国幅员辽阔,陆海兼备,地貌和气候复杂多样,孕育了丰富而又独特的生态系统、物种和遗传多样性。

（《中国的生物多样性保护》白皮书）

英语译文

China's land and sea territories are both vast; its complex terrain and diverse climate gave birth to unique ecosystems, abundant species, and rich genetic variety.

(Biodiversity Conservation in China)

> **┃ 解 析**
>
> 在本例的英语译文中,我们看到第二个分句中添加了代词"its"来指代前一句出现的"China",但中文原文中此部分并无代词。因此,即使是代词,在英汉语之间也不是完全对应的。

┃ 例1-2

中文原文

不忘初心,方得始终。

(《习近平谈治国理政》)

英语译文

Never forget why <u>you</u> started, and <u>you</u> can accomplish <u>your</u> mission.

(The Governance of China)

> **┃ 解 析**
>
> 此句的中文原文中并无任何代词,但英语行文需要明确的主语,因此翻译时必须添加代词。添加第二人称代词("you"和"your")有利于加强与读者的沟通,从而增强译文的可读性。

2. 名词的对应

┃ 例1-3

中文原文

刘家峧有两个神仙,邻近各<u>村</u>无人不晓:一个是前庄上的二诸葛,一个是后庄上的三仙姑。

(《小二黑结婚》,赵树理)

英语译文

In the village of Liujia Valley were two oracles, a man and a woman. Everyone in the neighboring <u>towns and hamlets</u> knew about them. The man was called Liu the Sage. The woman was called Third Fairy.

(The Marriage of Young Blacky, Sidney Shapiro 译)

> **解　析**
>
> 在此句中，"村"本来是一个没有多义和歧义的名词，但在英语译文中，沙博理（Sidney Shapiro）将其译为了 "towns and hamlets"，而没有译为 "village"。这主要是因为受到了上下文语境的影响。"刘家峁"在前一句中已被译为了 "the village of Liujia Valley"，因此本句中的"村"如果再译为 "village"，在英文中就有重复之嫌，故衍生为含义相近但概念范围更大的名词 "town" 和概念范围更小的名词 "hamlet"。

例1-4

中文原文

中国历来只是地主有文化，农民没有文化。可是地主的文化是由农民造成的，因为造成地主文化的东西，不是别的，正是从农民身上掠取的血汗。

（《毛泽东选集》）

英语译文

In China education has always been the exclusive preserve of the landlords, and the peasants have had no access to it. But the landlords' culture is created by the peasants, for its sole source is the peasants' sweat and blood.

(Selected Works of Mao Tse-Tung)

> **解　析**
>
> 此例的中文原文中，共有四个"文化"。但我们看到，前两个"文化"没有对应译为 "culture"，而是译为了 "education"。在汉语中，"有文化"实际上指的是"受过教育"，所以此处的"文化"译为 "education"，才是翻译了"文化"的真实意义，而不是字面意思。同时，将第一个分句译成 "in China culture has always been the exclusive preserve of the landlords"，也是不合乎逻辑的，因为每个社会阶层都有自己的文化，这不只是地主独有的。

例1-5

中文原文

杨克说，我也受你污染了，害得我一看史书就往西戎、东夷、北狄、南蛮方向看。我也越来越想跟狼交交手、过过招了。

（《狼图腾》，姜戎）

英语译文

Yang said, it's contagious. Now when I read history, I keep looking to <u>the barbarian tribes of the four corners</u> and am tempted to look for their connections to wolves.

(*Wolf Totem*, Howard Goldblatt 译)

解　析

在此句中,"西戎、东夷、北狄、南蛮"本身为专有名词,指我国古代居住在东、西、南、北四个方向的少数民族。在其英语译文中,葛浩文(Howard Goldblatt)未将东、西、南、北四个方向翻译出来,而是用了东、西、南、北四个方向的统称,将其译为了"the barbarian tribes of the four corners"。

3. 数词的对应

例1-6

中文原文

参观者们对本县的灌溉系统印象深刻,说是非常好,也对<u>一</u>年多以前才建立起来的农业研究中心,有深刻的印象。

(《通过翻译学英语》,李学平)

英语译文

The visitors were very impressed by this county's irrigation system, which they called superb, and also by the agricultural research center built only more than <u>a year</u> ago.

(《通过翻译学英语》,李学平)

解　析

在这里,"一"不能译为"one",即"一年多以前"不能译为"more than one year ago",因为"one"是数词,"more than one year ago"的意思是"两三年以前"。这很明显与中文原文中的意义不一致,"一年多以前"指的是"一年零几个月以前",所以这里的"一"要译为冠词"a"。

例1-7

中文原文

陈阵急忙下马,铲清扫净了雪。老人蹲下身,用小铁镐在冻得不太深的土地上刨出一个直径约40厘米、深约15厘米的圆坑,坑中还有一个小坑。

(《狼图腾》,姜戎)

英语译文

Chen dismounted and started digging in the snow, while Bilgee crouched down and scraped out a circle about a foot and a half across and a couple of inches deep with his little spade.

(*Wolf Totem*, Howard Goldblatt 译)

解 析

在此句中,葛浩文英译时将中文中习惯使用的长度单位"厘米"转换为了英语中习惯使用的"英尺"和"英寸"。因此我们看到,"40厘米"被译为了"a foot and a half","15厘米"则被译为了"a couple of inches",两者间只实现了大体的对应,而不是准确的对应。

例1-8

中文原文

熏不死,咱就用水灌洞,拉上十辆八辆木桶水车轮番往里灌,准能把小狼崽淹死!

(《狼图腾》,姜戎)

英语译文

Since we didn't smoke them out, let's see how we do with water. If we brought up nine or ten water wagons, we could drown every last one of those little bastards.

(*Wolf Totem*, Howard Goldblatt 译)

解 析

在中文中,"十辆八辆"类似"十个八个",是一种习惯性的半实指半虚指的数量说法。但在英语中,"ten or eight"则是一种听起来不合逻辑的说法,读者会奇怪为何要跳过中间的"nine"。英语中没有类似"十个八个"的说法,所以葛浩文将"十辆八辆"译为了"nine or ten"。

例1-9

中文原文

新兴市场国家和发展中国家面临相似的发展任务,深化务实合作,发挥互补优势,能产生"一加一大于二"的积极效应。

(《习近平金砖国家领导人厦门会晤重要讲话》)

英语译文

All emerging market and developing countries face similar tasks in development. By achieving deeper practical cooperation and tapping into complementarity, we can multiply the impact.

(Xi Jinping: Important Speeches at the BRICS Xiamen Summit)

解　析

在此句中,"一加一大于二"并不指数学意义上的加减运算,而是包含一种比喻意义,所以英译时没有翻译为数字,而是翻译出了其实质性的意义。

4. 搭配的对应

翻译实践中,在搭配层面也鲜少出现汉英完全对应的情况,即大多是部分的对应。

例1-10

中文原文

强调总依据,是因为社会主义初级阶段是当代中国的最大国情、最大实际。我们在任何情况下都要牢牢把握这个最大国情,推进任何方面的改革发展都要牢牢立足这个最大实际。

(《习近平谈治国理政》)

英语译文

It is important to stress the basic foundation of China being in the primary stage of socialism. This is the paramount reality and the most important national condition in contemporary China. We must always bear it in mind and promote reform and development in all respects on the basis of this very reality.

(The Governance of China)

解　析

在此例中,两个最高级修饰词"最大"都没有译为"the biggest",而是分别译为了"the paramount"和"the most important",主要是因为在英语中"the biggest"与"reality"和"national condition"不能搭配使用。

例1-11

中文原文

调动积极性是最大的民主。

（《邓小平文选》）

英语译文

When the people's initiative is aroused, that's the best manifestation of democracy.

(*Selected Works of Deng Xiaoping*)

解 析

在此例中，如果将"最大的民主"这一搭配形式直接译为"the biggest democracy"，会产生较多歧义，也会令人生疑。实际上，"最大的民主"在此指的是"最好的民主体现方式"，因此译为了"the best manifestation of democracy"。

例1-12

中文原文

抓精神文明建设，抓党风、社会风气好转，必须狠狠地抓，一天不放松地抓，从具体事件抓起。

（《邓小平文选》）

英语译文

To promote ethical progress and raise standards of conduct both inside and outside the Party, we must redouble our efforts and not relax them for a single day. And we should start by dealing with specific cases of wrongdoing.

(*Selected Works of Deng Xiaoping*)

解 析

汉语动词词义灵活多变，能与不同的词语搭配表达不同的含义，需根据上下文仔细揣摩。上例中，原文中的五个"抓"，根据不同的宾语搭配都有不同的译法，或是译为"promote""raise""deal with"，或是省略"抓"的含义，仅强调"抓"的方式，如"redouble our efforts"和"not relax them"。

▍例1-13

中文原文

中华文明历来崇尚天人合一、道法自然。

(《中国应对气候变化的政策与行动》白皮书)

英语译文

The Chinese people have always valued the idea that human beings are an integral part of nature and should follow the laws of nature.

(*Responding to Climate Change: China's Policies and Actions*)

▍解 析

此句中的谓语是"崇尚",译成"value"后其主语应为有灵主语,所以此处的"中华文明"应译为"the Chinese people",以符合英语中主谓需要保持一致的搭配要求。

5. 核心句的对应

▍例1-14

中文原文

治病必求于本。

(《黄帝内经·素问》)

英语译文

① The treatment of disease must follow this law.

(*Yellow Emperor's Canon of Medicine*,李照国译)

② To treat diseases, one must search for the basis.

(*Huang Di Nei Jing Su Wen*, Paul U. Unschuld & Hermann Tessenow 译)

③ In healing, one must grasp the root of the disharmony, which is always subject to the law of *yin* and *yang*.

(*The Yellow Emperor's Classic of Medicine*,倪毛信译)

④ In order to treat and cure diseases one must search into their origin.

(*Huang Ti Nei Ching Su Wen*, Ilza Veith 译)

> **| 解 析**
>
> 这是一个核心句,也可以说是简单句。但我们看到,谓语"求"和宾语"本"在四个不同的译文中分别被译为了"follow""search for""grasp""search into"和"law""basis""the root of the disharmony""origin"。这些译法都体现了谓语"求"和宾语"本"在汉语和英语中部分的对应。

| 例1-15

中文原文

心主脉,肺主皮,肝主筋,脾主肉,肾主骨。

（《黄帝内经·素问》）

英语译文

① The heart governs the vessels; the lung governs the skin; the liver governs the sinews; the spleen governs the muscles; and the kidney governs the bones.

（*Yellow Emperor's Canon of Medicine*,李照国译）

② The heart rules the vessels. The lung rules the skin. The liver rules the sinews. The spleen rules the flesh. The kidneys rule the bones.

（*Huang Di Nei Jing Su Wen*, Paul U. Unschuld & Hermann Tessenow 译）

③ The heart controls the pulse; the lungs control the skin; the liver controls the muscles and sinews; the spleen controls the flesh; and the kidneys control the bones.

（*Huang Ti Nei Ching Su Wen*, Ilza Veith 译）

> **| 解 析**
>
> 这是五个并列的核心句,谓语动词都是"主"。"主",即"主持""掌管"之义。在这三则不同的译文中,"主"分别被译为"govern""rule""control"。根据牛津英语词典的解释,作为动词,"control"的意思是"to limit sth. or make it happen in a particular way","rule"的意思是"(*often disapproving*) to be the main thing that influences and controls sb./sth.","govern"的意思是"to control or influence sb./sth. or how sth. happens, functions, etc."。因此,"govern""rule""control"三个词用来翻译此句中的"主"都不太合适。在此,用"be in charge of"或"be responsible for"可能会更适合些。案例中三种不同的译法都是与谓语动词"主"的意义的部分对应。

6. 文体的对应

文体对应也是汉英翻译中对应的重要内容。英语中有正式与非正式、文学与非文学、书面与口语等文体方面的区分。汉译英实践中,要尽量做到文体上的对应。

例1-16

中文原文

本宪法以法律的形式确认了中国各族人民奋斗的成果,规定了国家的根本制度和根本任务,是国家的根本法,具有最高的法律效力。全国各族人民、一切国家机关和武装力量、各政党和各社会团体、各企业事业组织,都必须以宪法为根本的活动准则,并且负有维护宪法尊严、保证宪法实施的职责。

(《中华人民共和国宪法》)

英语译文

This Constitution affirms, in legal form, the achievements of the struggles of the Chinese people of all ethnic groups and stipulates the fundamental system and task of the state. It is the fundamental law of the state and has supreme legal force. The people of all ethnic groups, all state organs and armed forces, all political parties and social organizations, and all enterprises and public institutions in the country must treat the Constitution as the fundamental standard of conduct; they have a duty to uphold the sanctity of the Constitution and ensure its compliance.

(*Constitution of the People's Republic of China*)

解 析

这段文字是法律文体,因此翻译时用词用句都要求保证正式性和严肃性。"最高的"译为"supreme",显得庄重严肃。"法律效力"译为"legal force","国家机关"译为"state organs",体现了术语的专业性和严肃性。"维护宪法尊严"的"尊严"和"保证宪法实施"的"实施"分别译为"sanctity"和"compliance",而非"enforcement"或"implementation",用词正式:"sanctity"强调神圣不可侵犯,"compliance"指遵守法律,与前文"各族人民""一切国家机关和武装力量"等主语相照应。

例1-17

中文原文

第三十八条 被监护人的父母或者子女被人民法院撤销监护人资格后,除对被监护人实施故意犯罪的外,确有悔改表现的,经其申请,人民法院可以在尊重被监护人真实意愿的前提下,视情况恢复其监护人资格,人民法院指定的监护人与被监护人的监护关系同时终止。

（《中华人民共和国民法典》）

英语译文

Article 38

Where a ward's parent or child, who has been disqualified as a guardian by the people's court for reasons other than having committed an intentional crime against the ward, and who has truly repented and mended his ways, applies to the people's court for being reinstated, the people's court may, upon considering the actual situation and upon the satisfaction of the prerequisite that the true will of the ward is respected, reinstate the guardian, and the guardianship between the ward and the guardian subsequently appointed by the people's court after the disqualification of the original guardian shall thus be terminated simultaneously.

(*Civil Code of the People's Republic of China*)

解　析

这一条法律规定是关于恢复监护人资格的。中文原文句式较长,文体较为正式,英语也译为了一个长句,结构严谨,与原文对应。

对应是翻译的基本思维方式,也是翻译的基本特质。没有对应,翻译就无从谈起。但从以上代词的对应、名词的对应、数词的对应、搭配的对应和核心句的对应来看,汉译英中的对应主要是理论上的或人们假设中的对应。实际上,在翻译实践中很难做到完全的对应。科勒(Koller,1979)提出翻译中的"对应"(correspondence)与"对等"(equivalence)两个紧密相连的核心概念。"对应"属于对比语言学的研究领域,主要比较两种语言系统间的异同,其考察的参数主要是索绪尔(Saussure)所指的"语言"(*langue*)层面的参数;"对等"则指具体的一个个"原语—目标语"的语言对等以及具体语境下的对等,其考察的参数主要是索绪尔所指的"言语"(*parole*)层面的参数。同时,科勒(1979)藉此区分了外语能力和翻译能力:对应方面的知识表明的是外语能力,对等方面的知识表明的才是翻译能力。关于"对等",科勒(1979)区分出了五种类型的对等:一是指称性对等(denotative equivalence);二是内涵性对等(connotative equivalence);三是语篇—规范性对等(text-normative equivalence);四是语用性对等(pragmatic equivalence);五是形式性对等(formal equivalence),即需要译者再创造的、有关语篇形式和审美方面的对等,也称为"表情性对等"(expressive equivalence),不同于奈达（Nida）提出的"形式对等"（formal equivalence）。这五种对等间存在一种等级关系，从指称性对等到内涵性对等、语篇—规范性对等、语用性对等和形式性对等，等级逐渐提升，可根据交际的需求，选取合适的对等类型。

当然，完全的对应或对等在翻译实践中都只能是一种理想，特别是在汉英翻译中。如果固守完全的对应或对等作为翻译实践的目标，实际上就是主张语言间的不可译性。我们应该对翻译持一种现实的态度。萨利斯（Sallis, 2002）对不可译性的界定就很实际，他认为没有一首诗，我们可以预先说其未来的翻译不配称之为翻译。如果说可以证明诗的不可译处甚多，那证明的只是一种更局限的不可译性。不论这些证明是如何架构的，说得多么无条件性，这样证明得出的诗的不可译性只是说诗经过翻译无法做到没有损失或没有由此损失所带来的变形和平整化。庞焱（2009）指出，任何文本都是能够传译的，但绝对完全的传译却是不可能的，因为原文文本是可译性和不可译性的对立统一。钟述孔（1997：149-150）指出，不可译论者倾向于以"绝对"的字眼讨论问题，他们倾向于坚持翻译不能有任何信息丢失，这种主张在理论上是先验的和形而上学的，在实践中是非建设性的；如果我们接受这种"无任何信息丢失"的标准，那么不要说翻译，就是所有的交流都无以为谈了。正如成仿吾（1984）指出的，翻译实践主要看能力与努力如何。换言之，人类的交流与沟通并非要求是百分之百精确的，而是允许存在一定的模糊区间，因此跨语言的翻译也不一定要求百分之百精确，虽然对应是其区别于其他交流方式的基本特质。

二、转换译法在汉译英中的应用

正是因为在翻译中无法实现完全的对应，也没必要实现完全的对应，所以汉英翻译中另一大母体性的翻译方法就是转换。到目前为止，我们认为在翻译转换研究方面，卡特福德（Catford）对翻译中转换的界定和分类都是最为系统的。

卡特福德（1965）在其专著《翻译的语言学理论》（*A Linguistic Theory of Translation*）中提出了翻译转换（translation shifts）的理论。"翻译转换"就是指翻译过程中发生的语言的改变。卡特福德（1965：73）将"翻译转换"界定为"从原语到目标语翻译过程中在形式对应层面上的偏离"。就翻译而言，卡特福德（1965）区分出了形式对应（formal correspondence）和文本等值（textual equivalence）两个重要概念。"形式对应"是语言系统层面上的概念，指涉的范围更广，即指目标语中的任何范畴（语言单位、语法成分、结构成分等）在目标语系统中占有的地位与其对应的原语中的范畴在原语中占有的地位尽可能相似，如英语中的名词"belongings"与西班牙语中的"*efectos personales* [personal effects]"；"文本等值"则主要指具体的"原语—目标语"语言对等，即指在具体语境下目标语的一个文本或文本的一部分与原语的一个文本或文本的一部分是等值的，如"he searched through my belongings"在翻译为西班牙语时被译为了"*examinó mi bolso* [he examined my bag]"。在翻译过程中，当"形式对应"和"文本等值"两个情形中的概念偏离时，就发生了"翻译转换"，如上面所说的"*efectos personales*"与"*bolso*"。

对于翻译转换的类型，卡特福德（1965）指出主要有两类：其一，层级转换（level shift），主要指的是在一种语言中用语法表示的概念，在另一种语言中则用词汇表示出来，如英语中的时、体等在中文中用词汇表示出来；其二，范畴转换（category shift）。范畴转换又可再分为四类：一是结构转换（structural shift），指的主要是语法结构的转换，如英语中"主语代词+动词+直接宾语"的结构"I like jazz"译为西班牙语时转换为了"间接宾语代词+动词+主语"的结构"me gusta el jazz"。这是翻译转换中常用的一类转换。二是词类转换（class shift），指的是译文用不同于原语的词类来进行翻译，如英语中的"a medical student"译为法语时转换为了"un étudiant en médecine"，英语中前置的形容词"medical"被译为了法语中后置的副词性修饰语"en médecine"。三是等级转换（rank shift），指的是原语和目标语在语言纵向上的句、小句、短语、词、词素等不同层级单位上的转换。四是系统内转换（intra-system shift），指的是原语和目标语虽具有较为相似的系统，但翻译时还需选择一个不对应的成分。例如，法语和英语在"数"和"冠词"系统方面类似，但英语的"数"和"冠词"和法语的"数"和"冠词"并不总是对应的，如英语中的"advice"是不可数名词，但在译为法语时需转换为可数名词"des conseils（复数）"；法语中"Il a la jambe cassée [he has the leg broken]"的定冠词"la"译为英语时转换为了不定冠词"a"，即"he has a broken leg"。整体而言，卡特福德（1965）认为，在翻译转换中，层级转换占少数，范畴转换占多数。卡特福德（1965）的翻译转换系统如图1-1所示。

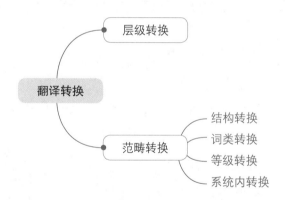

图1-1 卡特福德的翻译转换系统

下面，我们以卡特福德（1965）提出的翻译转换系统来分析汉译英中的转换问题。我们先看层级转换。根据卡特福德（1965）的观点，层级转换指的是原语中的语法内容在目标语中需用词汇表达出来。这种转换对英译汉来说是适合的，但对于汉译英来说则是相反的过程，即中文中的词汇内容需转换为英语中的语法内容，因为英语的形式性语法强，汉语的形式性语法弱。因此，在汉译英实践中，汉语中用词汇表达的语法内容往往就需要通过层级转换译为英语中形式性强的语法内容，这种层级转换主要体现在以下四个方面：时、体、态、数。

1. 时、体的层级转换

在时、体方面,汉语无形式化的语法,但英语有形式化的语法。因此,在汉译英中,需进行时、体方面的层级转换。

例1-18

中文原文

十八大以来的五年,<u>是</u>党和国家发展进程中极不平凡的五年。

(《习近平谈治国理政》)

英语译文

The five years since the 18th National Congress <u>have been</u> a truly remarkable five years in the course of the development of the Party and the country.

(*The Governance of China*)

解　析

在此句中,“是”不能直接译为“is”,因为原文中的时间范围是“十八大以来的五年”,描述的是一个从过去的时间点一直持续到现在的时间范围,在英语中应用现在完成时的语法形式来翻译,所以将“是”译为了“have been”。

例1-19

中文原文

海洋对于人类社会生存和发展具有重要意义。海洋<u>孕育了</u>生命、<u>联通了</u>世界、<u>促进了</u>发展。

(《习近平谈治国理政》)

英语译文

The ocean is of great significance to the survival and development of human society. It <u>gave</u> birth to life, <u>connects</u> the world, and <u>facilitates</u> development.

(*The Governance of China*)

解　析

在原文中,“孕育了”“联通了”“促进了”是三个并列的动作。但在英语译文中,“孕育了”用的是过去时,“联通了”和“促进了”用的是一般现在时,原因就是:“孕育了”发生在过去,必须使用过去时。

例1-20

中文原文

我把信取来一看，心里就突突的跳了几跳，原来我前回寄去的一篇德文短篇的译稿，<u>已经</u>在某杂志上发表了，信中寄来的是五圆钱的一张汇票。

（《春风沉醉的晚上》，郁达夫）

英语译文

When I got the letter my heart began to thump. One of my translations of German short stories <u>had been accepted</u> by a magazine, and I had got a money order for five dollars.

(*Nights of Spring Fever*，唐笙译)

> **解 析**
>
> 在此句中，"已经在某杂志上发表了"表示已经完成的动作。英语译文中用语法的表现形式进行了层级转换，使用过去完成时，译为了"had been accepted"。

例1-21

中文原文

中国的现代化建设刚起步，也许到本世纪末<u>可以看到</u>比较显著的进步，真正的进步要到下个世纪的三十至五十年。

（《邓小平文选》）

英语译文

We have only just begun the modernization drive. We <u>shall</u> probably <u>have made</u> considerable progress by the end of the century and even more notable progress 30 or 50 years after that.

(*Selected Works of Deng Xiaoping*)

> **解 析**
>
> 这段文字摘自1986年10月18日邓小平同志会见美籍华裔学者李政道教授夫妇和意大利学者齐吉基教授夫妇时的谈话。因此，这是从1986年看20世纪末要实现的目标，所以英语译文中用的是将来完成时，即"shall ... have made"。

2. 态的层级转换

英语常用语法被动态，少用意义被动态；汉语常用意义被动态，少用语法被动态。换言之,在汉语中,表达被动意义时往往不用被动语态的语法标记,但在英语中表达被动意义时一般要求使用语法标记。此外,在汉语中使用被字句时往往带有语义色彩,一般表示不幸或不如意的事,如"我被领导批评了一顿"。因此,汉译英时,需要进行被动语态的层级转换。

例1-22

中文原文

中央政治局集体学习,指中共中央政治局定期学习制度。由中共中央总书记主持并发表讲话,中央政治局全体成员参加,邀请有关部门负责人、专家学者,就经济、政治、历史、文化、社会、科技、军事、外交等问题进行专题讲解。

(《习近平谈治国理政》)

英语译文

The Political Bureau of the CPC Central Committee holds regular study sessions. The sessions are presided over and addressed by the general secretary of the Central Committee, and attended by all members of the Political Bureau. Leaders of relevant departments, experts and scholars are invited to lecture on economics, political science, history, culture, social affairs, science and technology, military and international affairs.

(*The Governance of China*)

解 析

在此例中,中文原文中没有一个"被"字,但在英语译文中有三个地方出现了被动语态"are presided over and addressed by""attended by""are invited"。这一段主要是对"中央政治局集体学习"这一名词术语的界定和阐释,因此选"study sessions"做英语句子的主语更能聚焦这一主题,也有利于句子整体的统一性,避免句子内主语的频繁更替(general secretary、members、leaders)。正是因为英语句子的主语选择了宾语性成分,所以后面的三个动词就需要使用被动语态的形式。

例1-23

中文原文

所有行政审批事项都要简化程序,明确时限,用政府权力的"减法",换取市场活力的"乘法"。

(《2015年政府工作报告》)

英语译文

Procedures and processes must <u>be simplified</u> and time frames must <u>be clarified</u> for all items requiring administrative review, and cuts to government power will <u>be made</u> to boost market vitality.

(*Report on the Work of the Government, 2015*)

解　析

与例1-22同理，中文原文中没有一个"被"字，但英语译文中有三处使用了被动语态："be simplified" "be clarified" "be made"。

例1-24

中文原文

到一九九七年还有十三年，从现在起要逐步解决好过渡时期问题。在过渡时期中，一是不要出现大的波动、大的曲折，保持香港繁荣和稳定；二是要创造条件，使香港人能顺利地接管政府。香港各界人士要为此作出努力。

(《邓小平文选》)

英语译文

There are 13 years left until 1997. We should start working now to gradually bring about a smooth transition. First, major fluctuations or setbacks <u>must be avoided</u>, and the prosperity and stability of Hong Kong <u>must be maintained</u>. Second, conditions <u>must be created</u> for a smooth take-over of the government by Hong Kong residents. I hope that people of all walks of life in Hong Kong will work towards this end.

(*Selected Works of Deng Xiaoping*)

解　析

在中文中，经常会使用无主语句。此例的中文原文就是一句无主句。英语译文中，第一句话添加了主语"we"，译为了主动句。但后面一句话中则将中文原文中的宾语转换为主语，使用了被动语态，增强了句子的客观性和无条件性。

3. 数的层级转换

在语法上，英语中的名词有可数与不可数之分，有单数与复数之分。同时，在英语中，名词的使用往往和冠词的使用紧密结合在一起。在使用英语的过程中，使用每一个名词时都要考虑是否需要使用冠词以及使用哪个冠词,因冠词是汉语中没有的词类。所以,汉译英实践中,需注意名词的数的层级转换。

例1-25

中文原文

对借外债要作<u>具体分析</u>。有些<u>国家</u>借了很多<u>外债</u>,不能说都是<u>失败</u>的,有得有失。他们由经济落后的国家很快达到了中等发达国家的水平。

(《邓小平文选》)

英语译文

As for <u>foreign loans</u>, we should <u>make a concrete analysis</u> of the question. Some countries have borrowed large <u>amounts</u> of <u>foreign funds</u>. This cannot be regarded solely as <u>a loss</u>; they have gained from it too, rapidly growing from economically backward countries into moderately developed ones.

(Selected Works of Deng Xiaoping)

> **解 析**
>
> "作具体分析"不能译为"make concrete analysis",因"analysis"是可数名词的单数形式,汉译英时需进行层级转换,添加不定冠词。"外债"译为"foreign loans"或"foreign funds",都使用了复数的语法形式,因一个国家所借的外债往往不止一种,所以需用复数。"失败"在此句话中译为了"loss",发生了转换,因为要和后文的"gain"对应使用。一旦选择了"loss",就要注意其单复数之别,借外债这种做法在此用代词"this"指代,因此"loss"需用单数形式,必须添加不定冠词"a"。

例1-26

中文原文

总之,今年的经济情况不错,比预料的还好。我们的改革是有<u>希望</u>的。

(《邓小平文选》)

英语译文

In short, this year's economic situation is good, better than we anticipated. The <u>prospects</u> are bright for our reform.

(Selected Works of Deng Xiaoping)

| 解　析

在此例中，"希望"译为了"prospect"，需转换为复数形式"prospects"。"prospect"既可作单数使用，也可作复数使用。作单数使用时，"prospect"表示的是"将要发生的事（a particular prospect is something that you expect or know is going to happen）"，如："There was a mixed reaction to the prospect of having new neighbours.（对于将要有新邻居这件事有多种不同的反应）。"作复数使用时，"prospect"才表示"希望"或"前景"，如："The prospects for peace in the country's eight-year civil war are becoming brighter.（在该国的八年内战中，和平的前景正变得越来越光明）。"

例1-27

中文原文

要综合运用货币政策工具，维护流动性基本稳定，合理引导市场利率水平，疏通传导机制，促进金融资源更多流向实体经济，特别是支持"三农"和小微企业。

（《2017年政府工作报告》）

英语译文

We will apply a full range of monetary policy instruments, maintain basic stability in liquidity, see that market interest rates remain at an appropriate level, and improve the transmission mechanism of monetary policy. We will encourage a greater flow of financial resources into the real economy, particularly in support of agriculture, rural areas, and farmers, and small and micro businesses.

(*Report on the Work of the Government, 2017*)

| 解　析

"综合运用货币政策工具"隐含着"会使用多种货币政策工具"的意思，因此英译时"工具"就要用复数形式"instruments"。"金融资源"一般也包含多种资源，所以英译用"financial resources"。"小微企业"在这里指的是全国亿万家小企业，因此理应用复数形式"small and micro businesses"。这些复数形式在中文原文中均没有体现出来，英译时需进行层级转换，以符合英语的语法要求。

由于中文和英文在数的语法范畴方面存在较大差异，汉译英时对数的语法范畴的解读有时也会有差异。下面是李煜的《虞美人·春花秋月何时了》这首宋词的两个不同版本的英译。

例1-28

中文原文

虞美人·春花秋月何时了

李　煜

春花秋月何时了，往事知多少。小楼昨夜又东风，故国不堪回首月明中。雕栏玉砌应犹在，只是朱颜改。问君能有几多愁？恰似一江春水向东流。

英语译文

① **The Emperor's Lament**

The fair spring flowers,

The autumn moons,

When will they cease to be?

The vanished past,

How much of it

Is wrapped in memory?

Last night the East wind shook

My roof again;

And I,

Beneath the moon,

Recalled

My hapless kingdom in the South.

The graven parapet,

The terrace of pale jade

Should still be there;

But all the carmine cheeks

Are changed.

You ask,

How much of sorrow is there left

Within my heart?

And I reply

A spring-tide river full

Of water, flowing East.

(*The Herald Wind: Translations of Sung Dynasty Poems, Lyrics and Songs*, Clara Candlin 译)

② **Yü mei jen**

Spring flowers, autumn moon, when will they end?

Of what once was, what's left?

Upstairs last night there was an east wind

Unbearable, in bright moonlight, to look back.

Carved railings, jade walkways, should be there still;

Only youth has gone.

How much more sorrow is to come?

It is a river, fed by spring rain, flowing east.

(*Beyond Spring: Tz'u Poems of the Sung Dynasty*, Julie Landau 译)

解　析

　　我们看到,在这两则英文译文中,译者对数的层级转换的处理各不相同。例如,对于"春花秋月",英国译者甘淋(Clara Candlin)译为了"the fair spring flowers, the autumn moons",都采用了复数,而美国译者兰道(Julie Landau)将"春花"译为了复数"spring flowers",但将"秋月"译为了单数"autumn moon"。"三春花开,中秋月圆",勾起了作为阶下囚的词人对往昔美好生活的无限追思,今昔对比,无比惆怅。甘淋将"秋月"译为复数,表达出原文中岁月不断更替、苦难无限的含义,突出了自然永恒与人生无常的强烈对比。对于"东风",甘淋译为了"the East wind",使用了定冠词"the";而兰道则添加了不定冠词"an",将其译为"an east wind"。对于"雕栏玉砌",甘淋译为了单数"the graven parapet, the terrace of pale jade",指代故国华丽的宫殿;而兰道译为了复数"carved railings, jade walkways",强调宫殿内具体的雕栏玉砌。

---

4. 结构转换

结构转换指的是语法结构的转换。由于英汉语言属于不同的语系,二者语法结构差异巨大,因此汉译英时结构转换较常用。

例1-29

中文原文

　　当前,世界多极化、经济全球化、文化多样化、社会信息化深入发展,人类社会充满希望。同时,国际形势的不稳定性不确定性更加突出,人类面临的全球性挑战更加严峻,需要世界各国齐心协力、共同应对。

(《习近平谈治国理政》)

英语译文

The world today is moving towards multi-polarity and becoming more economically globalized, culturally diverse, and IT-driven. All this offers hope to humanity. In contrast, however, instability and uncertainties are mounting, and the global challenges faced by humanity are ever more daunting, calling for joint responses from all countries.

(*The Governance of China*)

解 析

　　中文原文共两句话,呈并列关系("同时")。但在英语译文中,"同时"前后两部分的语法关系转换为了转折关系("in contrast, however")。在中文原文中,"需要"本是谓语动词,但在英语译文中转换为了非谓语动词形式,即"calling for"。在中文原文中,"人类社会充满希望"本是第一句话的一部分,但在英语译文中则单独译成一个独立句,这主要是因为话题发生了变化,在英语中需另起一句;此外,该句的主语也由"人类社会"转换为了"all this",以便与上文承接。因此,整体来说,此段话的英语译文与中文原文发生了较大幅度的结构转换。

例1-30

中文原文

　　草原的白天,若在无人的旷野或深山长途走单骑,只要手握套马杆,不管男女老少,就如手持腾格里的神符一样,可以在狼的天下通行无阻。

(《狼图腾》,姜戎)

英语译文

During daylight hours, a lone rider out in the wilds or up in the mountains — man, woman, old, or young — can travel undisturbed if he holds a lasso pole, almost as if it were a safe-passage tally given by Tengger.

(*Wolf Totem*, Howard Goldblatt 译)

解 析

　　在语法结构方面,英语译文取消了第一个假设关系"若",没有翻译。对于第二个条件关系,英语译文将结果部分转换到了条件部分之前。中文原文中的"就如手持腾格里的神符一样"用作前置状语,但在英语译文中转换为了后置状语。可见,这句话在英译过程中也发生了较大幅度的结构转换。

5. 词类转换

词类转换指的是原文中的词语在译入目的语时发生了词性转换。与英语相比较,汉语动态性更强,因此一般来说,汉译英时,汉语中的动词常常需转换为英语中静态性的名词、形容词、介词等。

例1-31

中文原文

在肯定成绩的同时,我们也<u>清醒看到</u><u>面临</u>的问题和挑战。

(《2022年政府工作报告》)

英语译文

While recognizing our achievements, we are also very <u>clear</u> about the problems and challenges <u>before</u> us.

(*Report on the Work of the Government, 2022*)

解 析

在此例中,原文中的动词性短语"清醒看到"在英语译文中转换为了形容词性短语"be clear about";动词"面临"转换为了介词"before"。两处分别将汉语的动态性表达转换为了英语中的静态性形容词或介词表达。

例1-32

中文原文

奶奶<u>披</u>着夹袄,送他们<u>到</u>村头。余司令说:"立住吧。"奶奶就立住了。

(《红高粱家族》,莫言)

英语译文

Grandma, a padded jacket <u>over</u> her shoulders, saw them <u>to</u> the edge of the village. "Stop here," Commander Yu ordered her. She stopped.

(*Red Sorghum*, Howard Goldblatt 译)

解 析

中文原文中的动词"披着""到",在英语译文中分别译为了介词"over""to"。在许多情况下,这种动词向静态性的名词、形容词、介词等的转换并不是绝对的,而是反映出一种语言使用的倾向性,有一个度的问题,即与英语相比较而言,汉语动态性更强,译者需要根据上下文语境、具体文本的体裁以及翻译目的等需要来决定是否进行转换。

例1-33

中文原文

当有殿头官喝道:"有事出班早奏,无事卷帘退朝。"只见班部丛中,宰相赵哲、参政文彦博出班奏曰:"目今京师瘟疫盛行,民不聊生,伤损军民甚多。伏望陛下释罪宽恩,省刑薄税,以禳天灾,救济万民。"天子听奏,急敕翰林院随即草诏:一面降赦天下罪囚,应有民间税赋悉皆赦免;一面命在京宫观寺院,修设好事禳灾。

(《水浒传》,施耐庵)

英语译文

① The officials discussed the situation in the Council Chamber and when the Emperor gave audience they all entered the Grand Audience Hall where they all kowtowed together. The appointed minister asked what business there was to bring before the Emperor, and the Prime Minister Chao Che, and the State Chancellor Wen Yen-po stopped forward. The former spoke, "Just now there is a serious pestilence in this Capital, and a great many people have died. I request that in your benevolence an edict be issued pardoning all criminals, reducing all sentences for future crimes, and lessening all taxes. We also beg Your Majesty to offer prayers to Heaven to save the lives of your people." The Emperor at once agreed to this, and added to the edict that in all temples there should be special prayers to Heaven to stop this great calamity.

(*The Water Margin: Outlaws of the Marsh*, J. H. Jackson 译)

② After the officials had made their obeisances, the chief of ceremonies cried:"If anyone has a petition, let him come forward. If there are none, this court will adjourn."

Zhao Zhe, the Premier, and Wen Yanbo, his deputy, advanced and said: "The plague is raging unabated in the capital. Victims among the soldiers and the people are many. We hope Your Majesty, in a forgiving and benevolent spirit, will reduce prison sentences and cut taxes, and pray to Heaven that the people be relived of this affliction."

The emperor at once ordered the Hanlin Academy to draw an edict proclaiming a general <u>amnesty</u> for all prisoners and canceling all taxes. He also directed that every temple and monastery in the capital offer prayers for a <u>termination</u> of the disaster.

(*Outlaws of the Marsh*, Sidney Shapiro 译)

③ Then the master of ceremonies shouted: "If there are matters to report stand forth and declare them; if not, take leave and depart." Accordingly the Prime Minister, Zhao Zhe, and the Chief Counsellor, Wen Yanbo stepped forward and said: "Your Imperial Majesty, a fearful plague is raging in the capital at the present time. There have been many losses among your subjects, both civil and military. We beseech Your Majesty, of your graciousness, to vouchsafe pardon to transgressors, to relax punishments and reduce taxes, and to offer up prayers and sacrifices for the <u>avoidance</u> of heaven-sent disasters and the <u>delivery</u> of all your people." The Son of Heaven, on hearing this petition, instructed the Imperial Academy to prepare forthwith an edict proclaiming the <u>remission</u> of prison sentences throughout the empire and the total <u>abolition</u> of general taxes and levies, and at the same time ordering all Buddhist temples and Taoist monasteries in the capital to perform the appropriate rites for the <u>prevention</u> of natural disasters.

(*The Marshes of Mount Liang*, John and Alex Dent-Young 译)

> **解　析**
>
> 　　通过对比《水浒传》这一片段的三版译文可以看到，从杰克逊（J. H. Jackson）、沙博理到登特—杨父子（John and Alex Dent-Young）的译文，呈名词化逐步增强的趋势。随着名词化的增强，译文也显得越来越正式，故事的节奏也随之放缓。

当然，也有相反的情况。有时，在汉译英实践中，也需将一些名词转换为动词，但这是少数情况。

║ 例1-34

中文原文

绿色是生命的<u>象征</u>，是大自然的<u>底色</u>。

(《中国关键词：生态文明篇》)

英语译文

Green <u>symbolizes</u> life and nature.

(*Keywords to Understand China: On Eco-civilization*)

> **解　析**
>
> 　　在此例中，两个名词"象征""底色"译为了动词"symbolize"，将具有相近意义的两个名词译为一个动词，使得译文更加简洁连贯。

例1-35

中文原文

　　清气在<u>下</u>，则生飧泄；浊气在<u>上</u>，则生䐜胀。

(《黄帝内经·素问》)

英语译文

　　① [If] *Qingqi* (Lucid-*Qi*) <u>descends</u>, it will cause *Sunxie* (diarrhea with undigested food in it). [If] *Zhuoqi* (Turbid-*Qi*) <u>ascends</u>, it will cause abdominal flatulence [or distension].

(*Yellow Emperor's Canon of Medicine*, 李照国译)

　　② When clear *qi* <u>is in the lower</u> [regions of the body], then this generates outflow of [undigested] food. When turbid *qi* <u>is in the upper</u> [regions], then this generates bloating.

(*Huang Di Nei Jing Su Wen*, Paul U. Unschuld & Hermann Tessenow 译)

　　③ If the clear *yang qi* <u>descends</u> instead of rising, problems such as diarrhea occur in the body. If the turbid *yin qi* <u>becomes stuck at the top and fails to descend</u>, there will be fullness and distension in the head.

(*Huang Ti Nei Ching Su Wen*, Ilza Veith 译)

> **解　析**
>
> 　　在此例中，三位译者在处理"在下"与"在上"两个介词性短语的英译时采取了不同的方式。李照国分别译为了动词"descends""ascends"；文树德（Paul U. Unschuld）与田和曼（Hermann Tessenow）的译文则与原文基本一致，也译为了介词性短语"in the lower""in the upper"；维茨（Ilza Veith）将"在下"译为了动词"descends"，但将"在上"译为了表变化的状态动词短语"becomes stuck at the top and fails to descend"，进行了内涵阐释。

　　在其他词类方面，因为在汉语中副词一般位于动词的前面，而在英语中副词一般位于谓语动词的后面，所以汉译英中存在着副词向其他词类转换的问题，如副词向形容词的转换、副词向介词短语的转换、副词向动词的转换。

（1）副词向形容词的转换

因为英语中存在"动词＋名词"形式的动词短语，汉译英时常把汉语中的动词译为"动词＋名词"短语，所以汉语中修饰动词的副词也被转换为了修饰名词的形容词。

┃例1-36

中文原文

二是扎实推进节能减排、生态建设和环境保护。

（《2011年政府工作报告》）

英语译文

Second, we made <u>genuine</u> progress in energy conservation, emissions reduction, ecological improvement and environmental protection.

(*Report on the Work of the Government, 2011*)

┃解　析

在中文原文中，"扎实"作动词"推进"的状语，是副词，但在英语译文中转换为了形容词"genuine"。这主要是因为"推进"译为了"make progress"，有了名词"progress"，就可以用形容词"genuine"修饰。

┃例1-37

中文原文

稳步推进医药卫生事业改革发展。

（《2010年政府工作报告》）

英语译文

We made <u>steady</u> progress in the reform and development of the pharmaceutical and healthcare fields.

(*Report on the Work of the Government, 2010*)

┃解　析

同例1-36，此例中，"推进"前的副词"稳步"在英语译文中也转换为了形容词"steady"，用以修饰"made progress"中的名词"progress"。

例1-38

中文原文

我们冷静地分析了中国的现实,总结了经验,肯定了从建国到一九七八年三十年的成绩很大,但做的事情不能说都是成功的。

（《邓小平文选》）

英语译文

We made a sober analysis of conditions in China and summed up our experience. We reaffirmed the great achievements scored in the 30 years from the founding of new China from 1949 through 1978, but that didn't mean that everything we had done was successful.

(*Selected Works of Deng Xiaoping*)

解　析

在此例中,中文原文中的副词"冷静地"在英语译文中被转换为了形容词"sober",用于修饰词组"made an analysis of"中的名词"analysis"。

例1-39

中文原文

要充分发挥传统媒体和新兴媒体的作用,广泛宣传资源环境国情和环境保护法律法规。

（《中国关键词:生态文明篇》）

英语译文

Traditional media and new media will be given full play in helping the public learn about China's true conditions of natural resources and relevant laws and regulations on environmental protection.

(*Keywords to Understand China: On Eco-Civilization*)

解　析

在此例中,中文原文中的副词"充分"被译为了形容词"full",是因为译文将"发挥"译为了名词词组,需要使用形容词修饰其中的名词"play"。

(2) 副词向介词短语的转换

由于状语本来就可用介词短语表示,因此在汉译英实践中自然可以把汉语中的副词转换为介词短语。

例1-40

中文原文

这样的巧合使父亲在此后的日子里,总是满腹狐疑地看着我和祖父,仿佛这场灾难是我们带来的。

（《在细雨中呼喊》,余华）

英语译文

This coincidence made my father look at me and Granddad with intense suspicion in the days that followed, for all the world as if we were the ones who had started the blaze.

(*Cries in the Drizzle*, Allan H. Barr 译)

> **解 析**
>
> 在此例中,译者将"满腹狐疑地"译为了介词短语"with intense suspicion",不但准确表达出了该副词的含义,而且使得译文简洁流畅、结构清晰。

例1-41

中文原文

我只能垂头丧气地走出屋去,用崇拜的目光去寻找哥哥孙光平。

（《在细雨中呼喊》,余华）

英语译文

I could only leave the room in low spirits and go off in search of Sun Guangping, whose feistiness I admired.

(*Cries in the Drizzle*, Allan H. Barr 译)

> **解 析**
>
> 在此例中,译者将"垂头丧气地"译为了介词短语"in low spirits",不仅表达出了"垂头丧气"之意,而且符合英语的表达习惯。

（3）副词向动词的转换

由于英语中的动词经常将动作的方式也包含在自身之中,所以汉译英时,汉语中的副词可以转换为英语中包含动作方式的动词。

例1-42

中文原文

父亲的伤口拆了线。父亲躺在窝棚里睡觉，母亲悄悄地溜进去，她轻手轻脚、脸皮滚烫。

（《红高粱家族》，莫言）

英语译文

Father's stitches were removed. Mother slipped into the shack where Father was sleeping and tiptoed up to his *kang*, her cheeks burning.

（*Red Sorghum*, Howard Goldblatt 译）

解 析

在英语译文中，中文原文中的两个副词"悄悄地""轻"分别被译为了动词词组"slipped into""tiptoed up to"。其中，词组"slip into"中含有"悄悄"之意，"tiptoe up to"中含有"轻轻"之意，因此译文将两个副词译为了动词词组，使译文更加地道。

例1-43

中文原文

尤其是妇人感情真挚，痴到无可形容，男子过了约定时间不回来，做梦时，就总常常梦船拢了岸，一个人摇摇荡荡的从船跳板到了岸上，直向身边跑来。

（《边城》，沈从文）

英语译文

Particularly the women, who were given to true infatuations of indescribable simplemindedness, would see their man in their dreams if he failed to return within the agreed-upon time. Often they'd envision the boat pull into shore and their man teeter on his sea legs down the gangplank, then come running directly to her side.

（*Border Town*, Jeffrey C. Kinkley 译）

解 析

"teeter"意为"（人）跟跟跄跄"，在此例中，译文将副词"摇摇荡荡的"翻译为动词"teeter"，并与介词表达"on his sea legs down the gangplank"进行搭配，不仅能够表达出原文的含义，而且使得译文结构更加清晰、紧凑。

例1-44

中文原文

但一听到客人进门说:"贺喜贺喜",心中有事,不敢再呆在屋门边,就装作追赶菜园地的鸡,拿了竹响篙唰唰的摇着,一面口中轻轻喝着,向屋后白塔跑去了。

(《边城》,沈从文)

英语译文

But when she heard the matchmaker say, "Congratulations, congratulations," at the door, she began to worry. Unwilling to squat by the front door any longer, she pretended to be shooing away the chickens in the vegetable garden. Flailing a bamboo whistling pole in the air, she softly scolded them as she ran toward the white pagoda in back.

(Border Town, Jeffrey C. Kinkley 译)

解 析

动词"flail"意为"用力地胡乱摆动",其中包含"唰唰的"之意,因此译文将"唰唰的摇着"译为了动词"flail"。

(4) 副词转换译法的综合应用

在翻译一个段落或一个语篇时,应综合使用副词的转换译法。

例1-45

中文原文

但是一切外国的东西,如同我们对于食物一样,必须经过自己的口腔咀嚼和胃肠运动,送进唾液胃液肠液,把它分解为精华和糟粕两部分,然后排泄其糟粕,吸收其精华,才能对我们的身体有益,决不能生吞活剥地毫无批判地吸收。所谓"全盘西化"的主张,乃是一种错误的观点。形式主义地吸收外国的东西,在中国过去是吃过大亏的。中国共产主义者对于马克思主义在中国的应用也是这样,必须将马克思主义的普遍真理和中国革命的具体实践完全地恰当地统一起来,就是说,和民族的特点相结合,经过一定的民族形式,才有用处,决不能主观地公式地应用它。

(《毛泽东选集》)

英语译文

However, we should not gulp any of this foreign material down uncritically, but must treat it as we do our food — first chewing it, then submitting it to the working of the stomach and intestines with their juices and secretions, and separating it into nutriment to be absorbed and waste matter to be discarded — before it can nourish us. To advocate "wholesale westernization" is wrong. China has suffered a great deal from the <u>mechanical</u> absorption of foreign material. Similarly, in applying Marxism to China, Chinese communists must fully and properly integrate the universal truth of Marxism with the concrete practice of the Chinese revolution, or in other words, the universal truth of Marxism must be combined with specific national characteristics and acquire a definite national form if it is to be useful, and in no circumstances can it be applied subjectively <u>as a mere formula</u>.

(Selected Works of Mao Tse-Tung)

┃ 解 析

　　在此例的中文原文中,标出了三处副词性状语,译文对这些副词进行了不同的处理。对于"生吞活剥地毫无批判地",译文省略了"生吞活剥地",因其义与"毫无批判地"重复;"形式主义地"转换为了形容词"mechanical";"公式地"转换为了介词短语"as a mere formula"。同时,我们看到,译文还添加了两个原文中没有的副词"first""then",增强了译文的逻辑性。此外,译文将原文第一句的最后小句"决不能生吞活剥地毫无批判地吸收"调整到了开头,符合英文先说重点的习惯,这是结构转换法的运用。因此,在翻译段落或语篇时,要综合运用转换译法。越是好的译文,转换应用得越多元、越恰当。

6. 等级转换

　　等级转换(rank shift),指的是在不同等级的语言单位上发生的转换,如短语转换为词汇、小句转换为句子等。在汉译英中,常见的等级转换有:短语与小句之间的转换、小句与句子之间的转换。

(1) 小句与短语、句子之间的转换

┃ 例1-46

中文原文

　　中国过去在很长的时间里处于封闭状态,<u>经济发展受到限制</u>,<u>直到一九七八年底我们党的十一届三中全会,才把这个问题恰当地解决了</u>。

(《邓小平文选》)

英语译文

China was closed for a long time, <u>which handicapped its economic development. Not</u>

until the Third Plenary Session of the Eleventh Central Committee, held at the end of 1978, did we solve this problem.

(*Selected Works of Deng Xiaoping*)

> **解　析**
>
> 　　我们看到，在中文原文中，该句由四个并列性的小句组成。但在英语译文中，这四个并列性小句的地位发生了等级转换：最后两个小句成为了一个独立句，而第二个小句则成为了第一个小句的非限制性定语从句。转换的原因是中文原文中的第三、四个小句讲的是另外一个话题，在英语中需单独成句；第一、二个小句间存在因果关系，所以需在英语译文中体现这种逻辑关系，在此选择使用定语从句体现两个小句间的因果关系。

例1-47

中文原文

　　智深正问间，猛闻得一阵香来。智深提了禅杖，趱过后面，打一看时，见一个土灶，盖着一个草盖，气腾腾撞将起来。智深揭起看时，煮着一锅粟米粥。

(《水浒传》，施耐庵)

英语译文

① As Sagacious was questioning the old monks he got a whiff of something fragrant. He took up his staff and went stealthily to the rear. There, on an earthen stove, steam was seeping through the reed cover of a pot. Sagacious raised the lid. Millet was simmering inside.

(*Outlaws of the Marsh*, Sidney Shapiro 译)

② While Zhishen was making these inquiries, an exciting odour was wafted to his nostrils. Staff in hand, he padded to the back to investigate. What met his eyes was a little earthenware stove with a woven cover, a fragrant steam spiralling up from it. He lifted the cover and there was a pot of gruel bubbling away.

(*The Marshes of Mount Liang*, John & Alex Dent-Young 译)

> **解　析**
>
> 　　在此例中，中文原文是一系列并列的小句。在两则英语译文中，我们看到登特—杨父子的版本中小句向短语的等级转换程度更高，有四处，分别是"staff in hand""what met his eyes""with a woven cover""a fragrant steam spiralling up from

it"；而沙博理的译文则只有一处小句向短语的等级转换，即 "through the reed cover of a pot"。但在小句向句子的等级转换方面，沙博理的译文转换更多，将原文译为了五个独立的句子，相对来说结构较为松散；而登特—杨父子则只将原文译为了四个独立句，结构更为紧凑。

▋例1-48

中文原文

香港自古以来就是中国的领土，一八四零年鸦片战争以后被英国占领。一九八四年十二月十九日，中英两国政府签署了关于香港问题的联合声明，确认中华人民共和国政府于一九九七年七月一日恢复对香港行使主权，从而实现了长期以来中国人民收回香港的共同愿望。

（《中华人民共和国香港特别行政区基本法》）

英语译文

Hong Kong has been part of the territory of China since ancient times; it was occupied by Britain after the Opium War in 1840. On 19 December 1984, the Chinese and British Governments signed the Joint Declaration on the Question of Hong Kong, affirming that the Government of the People's Republic of China will resume the exercise of sovereignty over Hong Kong with effect from 1 July 1997, thus fulfilling the long-cherished common aspiration of the Chinese people for the recovery of Hong Kong.

(*The Basic Law of the Hong Kong Special Administrative Region of The People's Republic of China*)

▋解 析

中文原文中由"确认"和"从而实现"所引导的两个小句，在英语译文中转换为了由"affirming"和"thus fulfilling"构成的两个动名词短语。转换之后，也体现出了该法律文本语言上的正式性。

▋例1-49

中文原文

当前，我国科技领域仍然存在一些亟待解决的突出问题，特别是同党的十九大提出的新任务新要求相比，我国科技在视野格局、创新能力、资源配置、体制政策等方面存在诸多不适应的地方。

（《习近平谈治国理政》）

英语译文

Currently, some prominent problems continue to interfere with China's scientific and technological development; they need to be addressed immediately. Our science and technology vision, framework, innovative capability, resource allocation, system and policies are not yet adapted to the new tasks and requirements set at the 19th CPC National Congress held in 2017.

(The Governance of China)

解　析

在此例中，"亟待解决的"在中文原文中只是一个短语，但在英语译文中则升级为了一个小句"they need to be addressed immediately"，起到了强调的作用，以突出解决这些任务的迫切性。中文原文为一个句子，但句内的第二部分在英语译文中单独成句了。

例1-50

中文原文

第一条　中华人民共和国为了扩大国际经济合作和技术交流，允许外国公司、企业和其它经济组织或个人（以下简称外国合营者），按照平等互利的原则，经中国政府批准，在中华人民共和国境内，同中国的公司、企业或其它经济组织（以下简称中国合营者）共同举办合营企业。

（《中华人民共和国中外合资经营企业法》）

英语译文

Article 1 With a view to expanding international economic cooperation and technological exchange, the People's Republic of China shall permit foreign companies, enterprises, other economic organizations or individuals (hereinafter referred to as "foreign joint ventures") to establish equity joint ventures together with Chinese companies, enterprises or other economic organizations (hereinafter referred to as "Chinese joint ventures") within the territory of the People's Republic of China, on the principle of equality and mutual benefit, and subject to approval by the Chinese Government.

(The Law of the People's Republic of China on Chinese-Foreign Equity Joint Ventures)

> **| 解　析**
>
> 　　中文原文中,有六个小句,但在英语译文中这些小句基本都转换为了介词短语,如"with a view to""on the principle of""subject to"。这样,就只保留了主句"中华人民共和国允许……",主次分明,逻辑清晰,避免歧义,符合法律文本对语言的要求。

(2) 小句与小句之间的转换

　　在汉译英中,等级转换,特别是小句与句子间的等级转换是使用频率很高的转换方式,因为在句式结构方面,中文习惯使用短的并列结构,而英语则习惯使用长的层级复合结构。当然,这种转换也受到文体方面的影响。在文学文体中,这种转换具有选择性,转与不转可以由译者的意图决定;在正式的非文学文体中,这种转换的必要程度则较高。下面,我们来看一个没有运用等级转换的例子。

| 例1-51

中文原文

　　历史一段一段。一朝兴,一朝亡。亡中兴,兴中亡。兴兴亡亡,扰得小百姓不得安生,碍吃碍喝,碍穿碍戴,可就碍不着小脚的事儿。打李后主到宣统爷,女人裹脚兴了一千年,中间换了多少朝代,改了多少年号,小脚不一直裹?历史干它嘛了?上起太后妃子,下至渔女村姑,文的李清照,武的梁红玉,谁不裹?猴不裹,我信。

(《三寸金莲》,冯骥才)

英语译文

Our history developed stage by stage. One dynasty rose; one dynasty fell. There were rises in the falls and falls in the rises. All the political ups and downs, harrying the common people, left them no peace and affected them in their homes, down to their very food, drink, and clothing. But all these upheavals failed to disturb foot binding. From the rule of Li Yu in 961 to the last Emperor Xuantong in 1912, women bound their feet for a thousand years. Even though dynasties changed, emperors changed, women's feet were continuously bound. So what difference does history make? From the empress and imperial concubine to the village girl and fisherman's daughter, from the great poetess Li Qing-zhao to the military heroine Liang Hong-yu, who didn't bind her feet? Only the she-monkeys, I'd guess.

(The Three-Inch Golden Lotus: A Novel on Foot Binding, David Wakefield 译)

> **解 析**
>
> 我们看到,在中文原文中,冯骥才用的都是些很短的小句,有的甚至就三四个字。其英语译文几乎也是由这种短句构成的,译者并没有将小句合并为语法单位上更大的句子。

叶子南(2019)指出,翻译中的转换是翻译的基本功。说起翻译中的灵活与变通,大家也许会说,就算是其他文本,比如科技法律方面的文字,翻译起来照样需要灵活与变通。没错,只要是翻译,就不可能亦步亦趋,紧跟原文。译者总得摆脱原文的束缚,根据译入语的习惯,写出译文读者读起来感觉顺畅的文字。在这个过程中,好的译者会展现高超的变通技巧,灵活地处理原文。

▣ 练习题

■ 1.译文补充

下列句子摘自《习近平谈治国理政》,其中都有"理念"一词,请根据具体语境将划线部分翻译为英文,注意对应与转换译法的运用。

(1)我们党以巨大的政治勇气和强烈的责任担当,提出一系列新理念新思想新战略。
Our Party has demonstrated tremendous political courage and a powerful sense of mission as it has developed new _____, new thinking, and new strategies.

(2)坚定不移贯彻新发展理念,坚决端正发展观念、转变发展方式,发展质量和效益不断提升。
We have remained committed to the new development _____, adopted the right approach to development, and endeavored to transform the growth model. The result has been a constant improvement in the quality and effect of development.

(3)必须坚定不移贯彻创新、协调、绿色、开放、共享的发展理念。
We must pursue with firmness of purpose the _____ of innovative, coordinated, green, and open development that is for everyone.

(4)加大全民普法力度,建设社会主义法治文化,树立宪法法律至上、法律面前人人平等的法治理念。
We will redouble efforts to raise public awareness of the law, develop a socialist culture of rule of law, and increase public awareness of the _____ underlying rule of law that the

Constitution and the law are above everything else and that everyone is equal before the law.

（5）我们秉持"两岸一家亲"理念，尊重台湾现有的社会制度和台湾同胞生活方式，愿意率先同台湾同胞分享大陆发展的机遇。

Guided by the _____ that we are all of the same family, we respect the current social system and way of life in Taiwan and are ready to share the development opportunities on the mainland with our Taiwan compatriots first.

（6）必须推进马克思主义中国化时代化大众化，建设具有强大凝聚力和引领力的社会主义意识形态，使全体人民在理想信念、价值理念、道德观念上紧紧团结在一起。

We must continue to adapt Marxism to China's conditions, keep it up-to-date, and enhance its popular appeal. We will develop socialist ideology that has the ability to unite and the power to inspire the people to embrace shared ideals, convictions, _____, and moral standards.

（7）树立安全发展理念，弘扬生命至上、安全第一的思想。

We will promote _____, and raise public awareness that life matters most and that safety comes first.

2. 句子翻译

下列句子摘自《习近平谈治国理政》，其中都有一个"观"字，请根据具体语境将下列句子翻译为英文，注意对应与转换译法的运用。

（1）社会主义核心价值观是当代中国精神的集中体现，凝结着全体人民共同的价值追求。

_____

_____

_____

（2）广泛开展理想信念教育，深化中国特色社会主义和中国梦宣传教育，弘扬民族精神和时代精神，加强爱国主义、集体主义、社会主义教育，引导人们树立正确的历史观、民族观、国家观、文化观。

_____

_____

_____

（3）坚持正确义利观,树立共同、综合、合作、可持续的新安全观。

_____

_____

_____

（4）中国秉持共商共建共享的全球治理观。

_____

_____

_____

（5）树立大食物观,发展设施农业,构建多元化食物供给体系。

_____

_____

_____

3. 段落翻译

以下段落摘自第三十四届韩素音国际翻译大赛竞赛原文,请将其翻译为英文,注意对应与转换译法的运用。

非物质文化遗产是中华优秀传统文化的重要组成部分,是我国各族人民宝贵的精神财富,体现着中华文明5 000多年的继往开来,需要进行系统性保护、传承与发展。不久前,第五批国家级非物质文化遗产代表性项目名录公布,一批具有重大历史、文学、艺术、科学价值的非遗项目列入了名录予以保护。截至目前,国家级非遗代表性项目已达1 557项。我国已建立起了具有中国特色的国家、省、市、县四级的名录体系,共认定非遗代表性项目10万余项。这既是非遗代表性项目名录体系建设的成果,也是中华文明与世界其他文明交流对话的重要资源。

_____

_____

_____

_____

第二章

拆分与整合

拆分与整合是两种相对应的翻译方法。拆分译法是指对原文复杂的语言结构单位进行层次划分,拆分为若干个较短、较简单的翻译单位。整合译法是指将两个或两个以上的语言结构单位进行合并,翻译为一个复杂的或结构紧凑的语言单位。其中,翻译的单位可以是各语言结构单位,通常包括句(短句、简单句、复杂句)和段两种语言结构层级。

在汉译英实践中,使用拆分与整合译法的原因与必要性在于英汉两种语言的句子结构差异。英语句子有严谨的主谓结构,主语不可或缺,谓语动词是句子的中心,两者协调一致,提纲挈领,聚集各种关系网络。因此,英语句子主次分明、层次清楚、严密规范,句式呈聚集型。汉语不受形态的约束,没有主谓形式协调一致的关系,汉语句子的主谓结构具有多样性、复杂性和灵活性的特点,因而句式呈流散型。英语重形合,注重形式接应,要求结构完整,因而严密规范,采用的是焦点句法;汉语重意合,注重意义连贯,不要求结构整齐,因而流泻铺排,采用的是散点句法。因此,根据英汉两种语言在句子结构特点方面的差异,在汉译英时,通常需要对语义上联系紧密的汉语句子的结构进行整合,使得译文结构紧凑;但同时也需要对冗长的汉语句子的结构进行拆分,以符合英语句子结构的特点和英语译文表达的需要。

此外,英语句子常用各种形式手段连接词语、分句或从句,表达语法意义和逻辑关系,注重显性接应,强调句子形式和结构完整;汉语句子少用甚至不用形式连接手段,通过句子中的词语或分句的含义表达语法意义和体现逻辑关系,注重隐形连贯,强调逻辑顺序和功能意义。英语注重形合、结构和形式,汉语注重意合、功能和意义。汉译英时,通常要先分析中文句子的功能和意义,才能确定其结构和形式,再根据结构和形式进行整合和拆分翻译。

因此,在汉译英中使用整合和拆分翻译方法的目的是使译文的结构紧凑、意义明晰、层次分明、脉络清楚,句子结构更符合英语语言的特点和表达习惯。本章将以汉译英实践中的经典案例,分析拆分译法、整合译法以及拆分与整合综合译法在汉译英中的应用。

一、拆分译法在汉译英中的应用

在汉译英翻译实践中,对于是否采用拆分译法以及在何种情况下进行拆分翻译,可以根据汉语原文的语义信息分布、句法结构以及标点符号的使用、语段结构、文本效果和风格等因素进行分析,通常将拆分的必要性而不是拆分的可能性作为基本的判断依据。在翻译时,可以对汉语原文中的一个短句、一个简单句或复句,甚至是一个语段进行拆分,译为英语的若干个短句、复合句、语段,或者是英语句子的主语、谓语、定语、状语等不同语法成分。

由于汉语注重内在意义而不注重外在形式,汉语的句型难以像英语那样以谓语动词为中心从形式上进行划分。英语重形合,较宜以语法成分为主、功能意义为辅来划分句型;汉语重意合,较宜以功能意义为主、语法成分为辅来划分句型。连淑能(1993)指出,按照表意功能以及表达形式,汉语句型主要分为九大类,分别为:①话题句,其基本形式是"话题语+评论语";②施事句,其基本形式是"施事语+动作语";③关系句,即表达各种逻辑语义关系的复句;④呼叹句,即在交谈中相互呼唤、应对或感叹的句子;⑤祈使句;⑥存现句;⑦有无句;⑧描写句,其基本形式是"主题语+描写语";⑨说明句,其基本形式是"主题语+说明语"。

此外,古代汉语不使用标点符号,相比于英语,现代汉语的逗号使用规则比较松散,使用频率较高,因此翻译时需考虑在逗号处拆分句子的问题。刘重德(1991)指出,一般而言,有五种汉语句子中的逗号转换为英语句子中的句号的情况,包括疑问分句前的逗号、概括分句前的逗号、对比分句前的逗号、解释分句前的逗号,以及举例分句前的逗号。

根据汉语原文的语义信息分布、句型结构以及标点符号的用法等,拆分译法通常在以下七种情况下使用。

1. 在总述—分述处拆分

汉语中有些句子习惯先作概括,即先总述,再分述;有些句子则先详尽阐述,再作概括,即先分述,再总述。总述与分述之间并不使用句号隔开,译成英语时,为使译文内容层次清晰,可以将总述与分述拆分为两个句子分别翻译。汉语的话题句、描写句和说明句等句型适用于此种拆分情况,通常在概括分句、解释分句或者举例分句前的逗号处进行拆分。

例2-1

中文原文

我们这一代共产党人一定要承前启后、继往开来,把我们的党建设好,团结全体中华儿女把我们国家建设好,把我们民族发展好,继续朝着中华民族伟大复兴的目标奋勇前进。

(《习近平谈治国理政》)

英语译文

Our generation of Communists should draw on past progress and chart a new course for the future. We should strengthen Party building, rally all the sons and daughters of the Chinese nation around us in a common effort to build our country and develop our nation, and continue to boldly advance towards the goal of the rejuvenation of the Chinese nation.

(*The Governance of China*)

| 解 析

　　译文采用拆分译法,在原文的解释分句"把我们的党建设好"前面的逗号处进行拆分,将原文的一个话题复句拆分为两个英语句子,避免译文过于复杂冗长,使之符合英语的句式结构特点和语言表达习惯。

| 例 2-2

中文原文

　　人的头盖骨,结合得非常致密与坚固,生理学家和解剖学者用尽了一切的方法,要把它完整地分出来,都没有这种力气,后来忽然有人发明了一个方法,就是把一些植物的种子放在要剖析的头盖骨里,给它以温度与湿度,使它发芽,一发芽,这些种子便以可怕的力量,将一切机械力所不能分开的骨骼,完整地分开了,植物种子力量之大,如此如此。

(《野草》,夏衍)

英语译文

　　The bones of a human skull are so tightly and firmly joined that no physiologist and anatomist had succeeded in taking them apart whatever means they tried. Then someone invented a method. He put some seeds of a plant in the skull to be dissected and provided the necessary temperature and moisture to make them germinate. Once the seeds germinated, they manifested a terrible force with which he succeeded in opening up the human skull that had failed to be opened even by mechanical means. This story tells us how powerful the seeds of plants can be.

(*Wild Grass*,刘士聪译)

| 解 析

　　译文将原文的一个说明复句结构拆分为五个英语句子,避免了译文过于复杂冗长。其中,译文在原文的转折分句"后来忽然有人发明了一个方法"之前的逗号处、解释分句"就是把一些植物的种子放在要剖析的头盖骨里"之前的逗号处、概括分句"植物种子力量之大,如此如此"之前的逗号处进行拆分,符合英语句式特点和语言表达习惯,使得译文的逻辑结构更加明晰,避免了译文的繁冗,增强其可读性。

例2-3

中文原文

　　杭州是创新活力之城，电子商务蓬勃发展，在杭州点击鼠标，联通的是整个世界。杭州也是生态文明之都，山明水秀，晴好雨奇，浸透着江南韵味，凝结着世代匠心。

（《习近平二十国集团领导人杭州峰会讲话选编》）

英语译文

　　Hangzhou is also an innovative and vibrant city with booming e-commerce. One click of a mouse in Hangzhou, and you can connect to the whole world. Hangzhou is also a leader in ecological conservation. Its green hills and clear lakes and rivers delight the eye on sunny days and present a distinctive view on rainy days. Hangzhou is imbued with a charm unique to the south of the Yangtze River that has been fostered over many generations.

(Xi Jinping: Selected Speeches at the G20 Hangzhou Summit)

解　析

　　原文第一句先总述杭州是创新活力之城，然后举例分述当地电子商务蓬勃发展；第二句先总述杭州是生态文明之都，然后再举例分述杭州的生态文明现状。译文分别在原文第一句以及第二句的举例分句前进行拆分，使得原文的语义和逻辑结构明晰化，译文的语义逻辑关系更加分明。

例2-4

中文原文

　　北京冬奥会的筹办，加速了主办城市生态环境治理步伐，推动实施了一系列生态环境保护相关规划与行动计划，加大了治气、治沙、治水力度，实现了场馆建设与生态修复、赛区环境提升同步推进，极大地促进了京张地区生态环境质量提升，为体育运动与自然环境融合发展提供了宝贵的示范作用。

（《北京2022年冬奥会和冬残奥会遗产报告（2020）》）

英语译文

　　The preparations for Beijing 2022 have increased the ecological environment protection efforts of the host city and facilitated the implementation of a series of projects and action plans in this regard. Efforts to control air pollution, desertification and flood have been enhanced, and the work of venue construction has been associated with ecological restoration and environmental improvement efforts. Consequently, the environmental quality of Beijing-Zhangjiakou Region has seen an improvement, giving visibility to an example of integrated development of sport infrastructure and natural environment.

(*Legacy Report of Olympic and Paralympic Winter Games Beijing 2022 (pre-Games)*)

> **解 析**
>
> 原文先总述北京冬奥会推动实施了一系列生态环境保护相关规划与行动计划，然后分述具体采取的措施，最后总述实施生态环境保护相关措施所产生的效果和作用。译文基于英汉语言特点和差异，采用拆分译法，在总述与分述处进行拆分，把原文译为三个英语复合句，使得译文语义清晰、逻辑结构分明。

2. 在逻辑关联处拆分

汉译英时，通常在对比分句、转折分句和并列分句前的逗号处进行拆分，汉语的关系句等句式结构适用于此种拆分情况。

例 2-5

中文原文

然而我们的阿Q却没有这样乏，他是永远得意的：这或者也是中国精神文明冠于全球的一个证据了。

(《阿Q正传》，鲁迅)

英语译文

But our hero was not so spineless. He was always exultant. This may be proof of the moral supremacy of China over the rest of the world.

(*The True Story of Ah Q*，杨宪益、戴乃迭译)

> **解 析**
>
> 译文采用拆分的翻译方法，将原文的一个长句拆分为三个英语简单句。其中，译文在原文的对比分句"他是永远得意的"以及解释分句"这或者也是中国精神文明冠于全球的一个证据了"之前的逗号处进行拆分，使得译文语义明晰，在忠实传达原文语义的同时，也清晰地呈现出原文的逻辑结构。

例2-6

中文原文

距离实现中华民族伟大复兴的目标越近，我们越不能懈怠、越要加倍努力，越要动员广大青年为之奋斗。

（《习近平谈治国理政》）

英语译文

The closer we approach the goal the more we should redouble our efforts. We can afford no slackening. More importantly, we should encourage more young people to join the great cause of making the dream come true.

（*The Governance of China*）

解析

译文将原文中的三个并列分句进行拆分，翻译为三个英语句子，然而译文并不仅仅简单地将三个并列分句进行拆分，还调整了原文分句的顺序，将"距离实现中华民族伟大复兴的目标越近"和"越要加倍努力"合并，作为译文的第一句，而它们中间的"我们越不能懈怠"则拆分开来，译为了译文的第二句，并在第三个句子开头增译了"more importantly"，使得译文的语义结构更加明晰。

例2-7

中文原文

它是多么残酷的一只硕鼠啊，每时每刻，它都在身边凋谢、流逝，但我无法阻挡它。许多人曾经用盔甲或者假意来抵挡它，我曾经用一堵围墙、一扇关闭的门窗和一种拒绝的姿态来抗逆，但都无济于事，除了死亡——那一块葬身的石碑可以拒绝它，没有其他的方式。

（《私人生活》，陈染）

英语译文

As if being devoured by a huge, pitiless rat, time withers away moment by moment and is lost. I can do nothing to stop it. Many have tried armor or flattery to dissuade it; I have built walls and closed windows tightly. I have adopted an attitude of denial. But nothing works. Only death, the tombstone over our graves, can stop it. There is no other way.

（*A Private Life*, John Howard-Gibbon 译）

> **解 析**
>
> 译文在原文"但我无法阻挡它"和"但都无济于事"两个转折分句前进行拆分,并将两个转折分句单独译为一句,使得译文语义结构更加明晰;此外,译者将原文中"除了死亡……没有其他的方式"这一关联句进行拆分,将"没有其他的方式"单独译为一句,起到了强调的作用。

3. 在疑问和反问处拆分

在翻译实践中,通常在中文的疑问或反问分句前的逗号处进行拆分,目的是使译文结构清晰简洁,起到加强语气的作用。

| 例2-8

中文原文

薛姨妈因道:"你素日身子弱,禁不得冷的,他们记挂着你倒不好?"

(《红楼梦》,曹雪芹)

英语译文

① Aunt Xue, however, protested: "You've always been delicate and unable to stand the cold. Why should you be displeased when they're so thoughtful?"

(*A Dream of Red Mansions*,杨宪益、戴乃迭译)

② But Aunt Xue protested. "You've always been rather delicate and you've always felt the cold badly. Surely it was nice of them to think of you?"

(*The Story of the Stone*, David Hawkes译)

> **解 析**
>
> 杨宪益、戴乃迭的译文和霍克斯(David Hawkes)的译文都将原文中的疑问分句"他们记挂着你倒不好?"进行拆分,单独译为一个疑问句,避免了译文因句子过长而显得繁冗,同时也起到加强语气的作用。

| 例2-9

中文原文

老费:"老耿呀,我也不懂,他小嘴不停,是做县长的材料吗? 治大国如烹小鲜,五十年固守一句话就不错了;他半年讲了六十二场话,他都说些啥?"

(《一句顶一万句》,刘震云)

英语译文

"I don't get it. That tiny mouth of his never stops yakking. Is he really magistrate material? Governing a large country is like making fine food. A single phrase ought to be enough for fifty years, but he gave sixty-two speeches in six months. About what?"

(*Someone to Talk to*, Howard Goldblatt & Sylvia Li-chun Lin 译)

解　析

译文将原文中的疑问分句"是做县长的材料吗"和"他都说些啥"与前文进行拆分,单独译为一个疑问句,起到了突出强调的作用,也避免了译文的冗长,增强了其可读性。

例 2-10

中文原文

上届世界杯有章鱼保罗,不知道明年还有没有可以预测未来的章鱼?

(《习近平谈治国理政》)

英语译文

During the last World Cup we had Paul the Octopus. I wonder if there will be another octopus next year to predict match results.

(*The Governance of China*)

解　析

译文采用拆分译法,将原文中的疑问分句"不知道明年还有没有可以预测未来的章鱼"进行拆分,单独译为一个陈述句"I wonder if there will be another octopus next year to predict match results.",起到了突出强调的作用,也使得译文语义更加明晰。

4. 在强调和感叹处拆分

在汉译英实践中,通常在表达强调或感叹语气的分句前进行拆分,汉语的呼叹句等句型适用于此种拆分情况。

例 2-11

中文原文

我国很多重大科技成果都是依靠这个法宝搞出来的,千万不能丢了!

(《习近平谈治国理政》)

英语译文

We have made many noticeable achievements in science and technology this way. This practice must not be given up!

(The Governance of China)

解　析

　　译文在原文的强调和感叹处进行拆分,将感叹分句"千万不能丢了"单独译为一个感叹句"This practice must not be given up!",从而加强了强调和感叹的语气。

例2-12

中文原文

　　陈阵觉得狼的脚掌比狗脚掌大得多,他用自己的手掌与狼掌比了比,除却五根手指,狼掌竟与人掌差不多大,怪不得狼能在雪地上或乱石山地上跑得那样稳。

(《狼图腾》,姜戎)

英语译文

　　The wolf's paws were much bigger than a dog's; measuring one against his palm, Chen saw that they were about the same size. No wonder wolves run so effortlessly through snow and across rocky hills.

(Wolf Totem, Howard Goldblatt 译)

解　析

　　译文采用拆分译法,在原文表达强调感叹语气之处进行拆分,将感叹分句"怪不得狼能在雪地上或乱石山地上跑得那样稳"单独译为一个句子"No wonder wolves run so effortlessly through snow and across rocky hills."。这种拆分处理方式加强了强调和感叹的语气,也使得译文的结构和语义更加明晰。

例2-13

中文原文

　　只得又转了一步,仔细一看,可不是昨儿那个丫头在那里出神。

(《红楼梦》,曹雪芹)

英语译文

　　① He approached and looked more closely. It was she, yesterday's girl, standing there on her own, apparently lost in thought.

(The Story of the Stone, David Hawkes 译)

② He strolled round the tree and looked more closely. <u>Yes, it was the girl of the day before</u>, apparently lost in thought.

(A Dream of Red Mansions, 杨宪益、戴乃迭译)

| 解　析

　　霍克斯和杨宪益、戴乃迭都对原文进行了拆分翻译,在原文的强调分句"可不是昨儿那个丫头在那里出神"前进行拆分,将该强调分句单独译为一句话。这种拆分处理不但传达出原文"可不是"的语义,也加强了强调的语气,增强了译文的可读性和可接受性。

5. 在主语或话题变化处拆分

　　汉语复句中经常会出现多个不同的主语或话题;而英语的句子有严谨的主谓结构,只有一个主语或者只涉及一个主题。由于汉语与英语在句式结构方面的差异,汉译英时,通常需要在主语或话题变化处拆分,即在话题或者主语发生转换的分句前进行拆分,以使译文的句式结构紧凑,符合英语的语言表达特点。

| 例2-14

中文原文

　　许多时没有动静,<u>把</u>总焦急起来了,悬了二十千的赏,<u>才</u>有两个团丁冒了险,踰垣进去,<u>里应外合</u>,一拥而入,将阿Q抓出来;<u>直待</u>擒出祠外面的机关枪左近,他才有些清醒了。

(《阿Q正传》,鲁迅)

英语译文

For a long time nothing stirred in the temple. <u>The captain</u> grew impatient and offered a reward of twenty thousand cash. <u>Only then</u> did two militiamen summon up courage to jump over the wall and enter. <u>With</u> their co-operation from within, the others rushed in and dragged Ah Q out. <u>But not until</u> he had been carried out of the temple to somewhere near the machine-gun did he begin to sober up.

(The True Story of Ah Q, 杨宪益、戴乃迭译)

| 解　析

　　译文将原文的一个结构松散的复杂长句拆分为五个句式结构紧凑清晰的英语句子,避免了译文过于复杂冗长。其中,原文由若干个主语不同的短句组成,整个句子中含有"把总""阿Q""两个团丁"以及"其他团丁"等不同主语,译文在原文主语变化处进行拆分,使得译文符合英语句式的主谓结构特点。此外,译文在原文转折分句"直待擒出祠外面的机关枪左近,他才有些清醒了"之前的逗号处进行拆分,并增译了"but"这一转折衔接词,使得译文连贯流畅,符合英语语言的表达特点。

例2-15

中文原文

蒙古民族的先祖是黑龙江上游森林中的猎人,后来才慢慢进入蒙古草原半猎半牧的,狩猎是每个家庭的重要收入、甚至是主要收入的来源。

（《狼图腾》,姜戎）

英语译文

The Mongols' ancestors were hunters in the forests surrounding the upper reaches of the Heilong River who slowly migrated onto the grassland, where they lived as hunters-herdsmen. Hunting was a significant and often a major source of income.

（*Wolf Totem*, Howard Goldblatt 译）

解　析

原文的句子中共有两个主语"蒙古民族的先祖"和"狩猎"。译文在主语变化处进行拆分,将原句译为两个主语不同的句子,符合英语的句式表达特点,也使得译文更加简洁。

6. 连动式施事句的拆分

汉语的复句中经常会出现多个谓语动词,而英语的句子中只能有一个谓语动词。施事句是汉语的一个基本句型,其基本形式是"施事语+动作语",其中连动式施事句通常包含多个动作语或动词短语。由于英语的主谓结构限制了谓语动词的使用数量,因此在汉译英时,需要对连动式施事句进行拆分翻译,以使得译文符合英语的句式结构表达需要。

例2-16

中文原文

他此时又带了七八分醉,又走乏了,便一屁股坐在床上,只说歇歇,不承望身不由己,前仰后合的,朦胧着两眼,一歪身就睡熟在床上。

(《红楼梦》,曹雪芹)

英语译文

① Now Grannie Liu was seven or eight parts drunk and thoroughly worn out from all her walking. Seeing a bed in front of her, she sat down on it gratefully, to rest her feet. But though she intended no more than a few moments' rest, as soon as she had sat down, her weariness overcame her. Her head went down and her feet went up as though she was no longer in possession of them; a darkness closed over her eyes, and she sank back on the bed, fast asleep.

(*The Story of the Stone*, David Hawkes 译)

② Being still more than half drunk and tired from her walk, she plumped down on the bed to have a little rest. But her limbs no longer obeyed her. She swayed to and fro, unable to keep her eyes open, then curled up and fell fast asleep.

(*A Dream of Red Mansions*,杨宪益、戴乃迭译)

解 析

原文为由多个动词结构组成的连动式施事句,霍克斯和杨宪益、戴乃迭的译文都对其进行了拆分,分别译为四个和三个英语句子。这种拆分的处理方式避免了译文过于冗长,使之符合英语的句式结构表达需要。

例2-17

中文原文

武松走了一直,酒力发作,焦热起来,一只手提着梢棒,一只手把胸膛前袒开,踉踉跄跄,直奔过乱树林来。见一块光挞挞大青石,把那梢棒倚在一边,放翻身体,却待要睡,只见发起一阵狂风来。

(《水浒传》,施耐庵)

英语译文

The wine was burning inside him as he walked. With his staff in one hand, he unbuttoned his tunic with the other. His gait was unsteady now, and he staggered into a thicket. Before him was a large smooth rock. He rested his staff against it, clambered onto its flat surface, and prepared to sleep. Suddenly a wild gale blew.

(*The Outlaws of the Marsh*, Sidney Shapiro 译)

> **解　析**
>
> 　　译者基于英汉两种语言的差异和特点，采用拆分译法，对原文两句由多个动词结构组成的连动式施事句进行拆分处理，译为六个英语句子，避免了译文过于繁杂冗长，使得译文结构和语义更加明晰。

7. 段落的拆分

在汉译英翻译实践中，可以进行拆分翻译的单位不仅包括句子结构，也可以是段落。段落的拆分，指的是将汉语原文的一个段落拆分为若干个英语语段。在汉译英时，应该根据段落中句子之间的语义关系、段落的结构和功能以及文体风格等方面的分析，考虑使用拆分译法的必要性，以使译文结构更加简洁，语义更加明晰。

例2-18

中文原文

　　回首过去，全党同志必须牢记，落后就要挨打，发展才能自强。审视现在，全党同志必须牢记，道路决定命运，找到一条正确的道路多么不容易，我们必须坚定不移走下去。展望未来，全党同志必须牢记，要把蓝图变为现实，还有很长的路要走，需要我们付出长期艰苦的努力。

　　每个人都有理想和追求，都有自己的梦想。现在，大家都在讨论中国梦，我以为，实现中华民族伟大复兴，就是中华民族近代以来最伟大的梦想。这个梦想，凝聚了几代中国人的夙愿，体现了中华民族和中国人民的整体利益，是每一个中华儿女的共同期盼。历史告诉我们，每个人的前途命运都与国家和民族的前途命运紧密相连。国家好、民族好，大家才会好。实现中华民族伟大复兴是一项光荣而艰巨的事业，需要一代又一代中国人共同为之努力。空谈误国，实干兴邦。我们这一代共产党人一定要承前启后、继往开来，把我们的党建设好，团结全体中华儿女把我们国家建设好，把我们民族发展好，继续朝着中华民族伟大复兴的目标奋勇前进。

（《习近平谈治国理政》）

英语译文

Reviewing the past, all Party members must bear in mind that backwardness left us vulnerable to attack, whereas only development makes us strong.

Looking at the present, all Party members must bear in mind that the path we take determines our destiny and that we must resolutely keep to the right path that we have found through great difficulties.

Looking ahead at the future, all Party members must bear in mind that we still have a long way to go and much hard work to do before we can turn our blueprint into reality.

Everyone has an ideal, ambition and dream. We are now all talking about the Chinese Dream. In my opinion, achieving the rejuvenation of the Chinese nation has been the greatest dream of the Chinese people since the advent of modern times. This dream embodies the long-cherished hope of several generations of the Chinese people, gives expression to the overall interests of the Chinese nation and the Chinese people, and represents the shared aspiration of all the sons and daughters of the Chinese nation.

History shows that the future and destiny of each and every one of us are closely linked to those of our country and nation. One can do well only when one's country and nation do well. Achieving the rejuvenation of the Chinese nation is both a glorious and arduous mission that requires the dedicated efforts of the Chinese people one generation after another. Empty talk harms the country, while hard work makes it flourish. Our generation of Communists should draw on past progress and chart a new course for the future. We should strengthen Party building, rally all the sons and daughters of the Chinese nation around us in a common effort to build our country and develop our nation, and continue to boldly advance towards the goal of the rejuvenation of the Chinese nation.

(*The Governance of China*)

解　析

原文为两个段落。译文采用拆分译法，对于原文的第一个段落，在"回首过去""审视现在""展望未来"三个不同的时间表达处进行拆分，并根据这三个不同的主题，分别译为三个段落；对于原文的第二个段落，在举例分述处（"历史告诉我们……"）进行拆分，译为两个段落。这种处理方式使得译文逻辑结构更加清晰，避免译文繁冗。

例2-19

中文原文

原来这李氏即贾珠之妻。珠虽夭亡，幸存一子，取名贾兰，今方五岁，已入学攻书。这李氏亦系金陵名宦之女，父名李守中，曾为国子监祭酒，族中男女无有不诵诗读书者。至李守中承继以来，便说"女子无才便有德"，故生了李氏时，便不十分令其读书，只不过将些《女四书》《列女传》《贤媛集》等三四种书，使他认得几个字，记得前朝这几个贤女便罢了，却只以纺绩井臼为要，因取名为李纨，字宫裁。因此这李纨虽青春丧偶，居家处膏粱锦绣之中,竟如槁木死灰一般,一概无见无闻,唯知侍亲养子,外则陪侍小姑等针黹^①诵读而已。今黛玉虽客寄于斯,日有这般姐妹相伴,除老父外,余者也都无庸虑及了。

(《红楼梦》,曹雪芹)

英语译文

① Li Wan was the widow of Jia Zhu who had died young, but luckily she had a son, Jia Lan, just five and already in school. Her father, Li Shouzhong, a notable of Jinling, had served as a Libationer in the Imperial College. All the sons and daughters of his clan had been devoted to the study of the classics.

When he became head of the family, however, in the belief that "an unaccomplished woman is a virtuous woman," instead of making his daughter study hard he simply had her taught enough to read a few books such as *The Four Books for Girls*, *Biographies of Martyred Women*, and *Lives of Exemplary Ladies* so that she might remember the deeds of worthy women of earlier dynasties while devoting her main attention to weaving and household tasks. That was why he gave her the name Li Wan and the courtesy name Gongcai.

So this young widow living in the lap of luxury was no better off than withered wood or cold ashes, taking no interest in the outside world. Apart from waiting on her elders and looking after her son, all she did was to accompany the girls at their embroidery or reading.

Though Daiyu was only a guest here, with cousins like these to keep her company she felt completely at home, except for worrying sometimes about her father.

(*A Dream of Red Mansions*,杨宪益、戴乃迭译)

② Li Wan's husband Jia Zhu had died young, but fortunately not without issue. He left her a son called Jia Lan who was now just five years' old and had already begun his schooling. Like most of the Jia women, Li Wan was the daughter of a distinguished Nanking official. Her father, Li Shou-zhong, had been a Director of Education.

Up to Li Shou-zhong's time, all members of the clan, including the women, had been given a first-class education; but when Li Shou-zhong became head of the family, he founded his educational policy for girls on the good old maxim "a stupid woman is a virtuous one" and, when he had a daughter of his own, refused to let her engage in serious study. She was permitted to work her way through *The Four Books for Girls* and *Lives of Noble Women*, so that she might be able to recognize a few characters and be familiar with some of the models of female virtue of former ages; but overriding importance was to be attached to spinning and

---

① 黹:读 zhǐ,旧时妇女针线活儿的总称。

sewing, and even her name "Wan", which means a kind of silk, was intended to symbolize her dedication to the needle.

Thanks to her upbringing, this young widow living in the midst of luxury and self-indulgence was able to keep herself like the "withered tree and dead ashes" of the philosopher, shutting out everything that did not concern her and attending only to the duties of serving her husband's parents and bringing up her child. Whatever leisure this left her was devoted to her little sister-in-law and cousins, accompanying them at their embroidery or hearing them recite their lessons.

With such gentle companions to console her, Dai-yu, though a stranger and far from home, soon had nothing apart from her old father that she needed worry about.

(*The Story of the Stone*, David Hawkes 译)

| 解 析

　　杨宪益、戴乃迭和霍克斯的译文都对原文语段进行了拆分,译为四个段落。杨宪益、戴乃迭的译文分别在转折逻辑关系衔接处"至李守中承继以来"、因果关系衔接处"因此这李纨……"以及主语转换处"今黛玉虽客寄于斯"进行拆分;霍克斯的译文在主题转换处"族中男女无有不诵诗读书者"、因果关系衔接处"因此这李纨……"以及主语转换处"今黛玉虽客寄于斯……"进行拆分。两则译文的译者使用拆分译法,使得译文结构更加清晰,可读性和可接受性增强。

| 例2-20

中文原文

　　且说东京开封府汴梁宣武军,一个浮浪破落户子弟,姓高,排行第二,自小不成家业,只好刺枪使棒,最是踢得好脚气毬。京师人口顺,不叫高二,却都叫他做高毬。后来发迹,便将气毬那字去了毛傍,添作立人,便改作姓高名俅。这人吹弹歌舞,刺枪使棒,相扑顽耍,颇能诗书词赋;若论仁义礼智,信行忠良,却是不会。只在东京城里城外帮闲。因帮了一个生铁王员外儿子使钱,每日三瓦两舍,风花雪月,被他父亲开封府里告了一纸文状。府尹把高俅断了二十脊杖,迭配出界发放。东京城里人民,不许容他在家宿食。高俅无计奈何,只得来淮西临淮州投奔一个开赌坊的闲汉柳大郎,名唤柳世权。他平生专好惜客养闲人,招纳四方干隔涝汉子①。

(《水浒传》,施耐庵)

---

① 干隔涝汉子:比喻不干不净、不三不四的人。

英语译文

In Bianliang the Eastern Capital, in Kaifeng Prefecture previously called Xuanwu District, there lived a young scamp named Gao. A second son, he was quite useless. He cared only for jousting with spear and staff, and was an excellent football player. People in the capital were fond of making quips. They dubbed him Gao Qiu, or "Gao the Ball." Later, when he prospered, he changed "Qiu" to another character with the same sound but with a less inelegant meaning.

In addition to his skill with weapons, Gao Qiu could play musical instruments and sing and dance. He also learned a bit about poetry and versifying. But when it came to virtue and proper behavior, he didn't know a thing. He spent his time gadding about the city and its environs. Thanks to him, the son of Master Wang, an iron-shop owner, dissipated a considerable sum of money in theaters, gambling dens and brothels.

For this reason the father made a written complaint against Gao to Kaifeng Prefecture. The prefect gave Gao twenty strokes, banished him from the city, and forbade the people of the Eastern Capital from either feeding him or giving him shelter. Gao Qiu's solution was to proffer his services to one Liu Shiquan, known as Liu the Eldest, who ran a gambling house in Linhuai Prefecture, west of the Huaihe River. Liu surrounded himself with idlers and riffraff from all over.

(*The Outlaws of the Marsh*, Sideny Shapiro 译)

| 解　析

　　沙博理采用拆分译法,分别在语义衔接处"这人吹弹歌舞,刺枪使棒"和"被他父亲开封府里告了一纸文状"进行拆分,将原文一个段落拆分为三个段落,使得译文结构简洁、语义逻辑清晰,同时也避免了译文的冗长和繁杂。

| 例2-21

中文原文

　　然而这一夜,举人老爷反而不能睡:他和把总呕了气了。举人老爷主张第一要追赃,把总主张第一要示众。把总近来很不将举人老爷放在眼里了,拍案打凳的说道,"惩一儆百! 你看,我做革命党还不上二十天,抢案就是十几件,全不破案,我的面子在那里? 破了案,你又来迁。不成! 这是我管的!"举人老爷窘急了,然而还坚持,说是倘若不追赃,他便立刻辞了帮办民政的职务。而把总却道,"请便罢!"于是举人老爷在这一夜竟没有睡，但幸而第二天倒也没有辞。

(《阿Q正传》，鲁迅)

英语译文

That night, however, the successful provincial candidate was unable to go to sleep, because he had quarrelled with the captain. The successful provincial candidate had insisted that the most important thing was to recover the stolen goods, while the captain said the most important thing was to make a public example. Recently the captain had come to treat the successful provincial candidate quite disdainfully. So, banging his fist on the table, he said, "Punish one to awe one hundred! See now, I have been a member of the revolutionary party for less than twenty days, but there have been a dozen cases of robbery, none of them solved yet; and think how badly that reflects on me. Now this one has been solved, you come and argue like a pedant. It won't do! This is my affair."

The successful provincial candidate was very upset, but he still persisted, saying that if the stolen goods were not recovered, he would resign immediately from his post as assistant civil administrator. "As you please!" said the captain.

In consequence the successful provincial candidate did not sleep that night, but happily he did not hand in his resignation the next day after all.

(*The True Story of Ah Q*，杨宪益、戴乃迭译)

解 析

译文根据原文语段中句子之间的语义关系，将原文拆分为三个段落，使得译文的结构层次更加清晰、连贯、分明，同时这种拆分翻译方法也避免了译文的冗长。

例2-22

中文原文

千年古都，古都千年，也是一部玉的历史。它曾经集中了多少珍宝，养育了多少巧匠，创造了多少奇迹！北海团城承光殿前的"渎山大玉海"，已见元大都玉器行业的端倪。这件大玉海，原在琼岛广寒殿中，是元世祖忽必烈大宴群臣时的贮酒器，以大块整玉雕成，沉雄博大，气势磅礴，重三千五百斤，可贮酒三十余担，为世所罕见的巨型玉器和艺术珍品，历时十五年雕琢而成，从金至元，跨了两个朝代！明代官府的御用监广召艺人进京，琢玉行业日趋繁荣，到清代雍正、乾隆年间，已达鼎盛，并且进行明确分工，琢玉、碾玉、抛光都有专门的作坊，日夜为皇室官府赶制玩物、饰物和日用品，凡瓶、炉、卣①、鼎、觚，首饰、衣饰、车饰、马饰，餐具、酒具等等无所不包，还在如意馆设雕玉作，专为玉玺、玉册刻字。清朝末年，内忧外患，玉器行业趋于消沉，至第一次世界大战结束，欧洲、日本经济复苏，对工艺品的需求刺激了北京的玉器生产，形成了自18世纪末开始的玉器出口贸易的高潮时期。到了民国初期，北京的珠宝玉石已有四十余家，琢磨玉石的作坊三十余家，古玩铺百余家，在崇文门外的花市一带和前门外廊房二条、三条、炭儿胡同、羊肉胡同，终日不绝于耳的是"沙沙"的磨玉之声，玉器行手工艺人已达六千之余！比较著名的作坊有：崇文门外的宝珍斋、东四牌楼的德宝斋、羊市大街的富润斋、廊房二条的魁星斋，随之又崛起义珍荣、天珍斋、济兴成等等。那时的奇珍斋还在惨淡经营，名声甚微，根本无力跻身于强者之列，只在廊房二条开一个小小的"连家铺"，前面两间门脸儿，算是作坊，后头连着几间房屋，全家居住。因为店小，虽有一块由"玉魔"老人题字的大匾，却一直没在门前悬挂，除了有生意来往的行里人，一般人只当这里是普通住家。

（《穆斯林的葬礼》,霍达）

英语译文

　　The history of this ancient capital, millenniums old, is also a history of jades, for the city had amassed countless gems, nourished artisans without number, and created no end of miracles. The vast Dushan jade-jar kept in front of the Chengguangdian Hall in the Circular City at Beihai Park is a standing testimony of the emergent jade craftsmanship in the Yuan Capital Dadu. Reputed to be the wine jar used by Kublai Khan in entertaining his courtiers, weighing 3,500 *jin* and having a capacity of over 30 *dan*, the grand vessel was carved out of one huge jade boulder and is as impressive as it is gigantic. Rare for its size and artistic craftsmanship, this tour de force is said to have taken fifteen years to carve, spanning two dynasties, the Jin and the Yuan.

　　In the Ming Dynasty, when the country's best lapidarists were assembled in the palace workshops, the jade craft began to flourish, reaching its zenith during the reigns of the Qing emperors Yongzheng and Qianlong. By then there was distinct division of labour — grinding or polishing the stones. Day and night the craftsmen were engaged in making wares for the court — bric-a-brac both decorative and those for daily use, jewellery, accessories for dress, carriages and horses, dinnerware, wine sets and innumerable others. In addition, an engraving workshop was set at Ruyiguan Hall that specialized in carving royal seals and

① 卣：古代的一种盛酒器具，口小腹大，有盖和提梁。

jade tablets (sacrificial objects used by royalty). But in the late Qing period, when China was torn by internal strife and foreign invasion, the jade craft declined. The rising international demand for handicraft products consequent to the revival of the European and Japanese economies after the conclusion of the First World War gave impetus to Beijing's jade craft industry and pushed China's jadeware export business, begun in the late 18th century, to its peak. By the early years of the Republic Beijing boasted of more than forty stores dealing in jade and other precious stones, over thirty jade workshops and some one hundred antique shops. The sound of drilling and grinding could be heard all day long in Flower Street outside Chongwenmen Gate and in Langfang Lanes One and Two beyond the Qianmen Gate, the number of lapidaries having exceeded six thousand.

At that time the Rare Gem Studio was a small and insignificant workshop with very little business and absolutely no hope of ever entering the rank of large establishments. Located in Langfang Lane Two, this small cottage-industry had only two front rooms for the workshop and a few rooms at the back as family quarters. Though it had a name, it had no signboard on the door. Except for those who had dealings with it, people took it to be a mere residence.

(*The Jade King: History of a Chinese Muslim Family*，关月华、钟良弼译)

┃ 解 析

原文语段叙述了古都玉的历史，并按时间顺序分别阐述了不同历史阶段古都玉的发展情况。译者采用拆分译法，一方面在时间由元代过渡到明代处进行拆分；另一方面，当原文的主题转至谈论奇珍斋时，译者也对原文进行了拆分。总之，译文将原文的一个段落拆分为三个段落，使之结构简洁、语义明晰，可读性增强。此外，译文省译了"炭儿胡同、羊肉胡同"两处地名和"宝珍斋""德宝斋"等作坊名称，因为它们对译文读者来说意义不大，省译后也使得译文更加简洁。关于省略译法的详细说明，请参见本书第四章。

二、整合译法在汉译英中的应用

整合译法是与拆分译法相对应的翻译方法。在汉译英翻译实践中，既然存在拆分现象，也就存在整合现象。汉语句子结构具有多样性、复杂性和灵活性，因而汉语句式呈流散型；英语句子结构受主谓结构的限制，句式呈聚集型。由于英汉语言结构之间的差异，在汉译英实践中应用整合译法的目的是使英语译文的结构衔接更加紧凑连贯，避免出现结构过于松散或者语义重复的英语译文。根据汉语原文的语义信息分布和英汉语言的句型结构特点等，整合译法常在以下三种情况下使用。

1. 在主语或话题相同处整合

相邻的两个或若干个汉语短句或复句通常具有同一主语，或者涉及同一话题。在汉译英时，通常可以将带有相同主语或相同话题的句子进行整合，译为一个结构紧凑的英语复杂句，以避免语义重复，符合英语的句式表达要求。

▌例2-23

中文原文

　　作为最早签署和批准《生物多样性公约》的缔约方之一，中国一贯高度重视生物多样性保护，不断推进生物多样性保护与时俱进、创新发展，取得显著成效，走出了一条中国特色生物多样性保护之路。

（《中国的生物多样性保护》白皮书）

英语译文

　　China, as one of the first countries to sign and approve the Convention on Biological Diversity, has always attached great importance to biodiversity conservation and preserves biodiversity with creative and up-to-date measures, achieving substantial progress on a distinctively Chinese path of conservation.

(*Biodiversity Conservation in China*)

> **解　析**
> 　　译文将原文具有同一主语"中国"的分句进行整合，用英语的介词短语和非谓语等句式结构，译为一个结构紧凑连贯的英语复杂句，使得译文符合英语的语言表达特点和习惯。

▌例2-24

中文原文

　　一日，炎夏永昼，士隐于书房闲坐，至手倦抛书，伏几少憩，不觉朦胧睡去。

（《红楼梦》，曹雪芹）

英语译文

　　One long hot summer day as Shih-yin was sitting idly in his study, the book slipped from his hand and, leaning his head on the desk, he fell asleep.

(*A Dream of Red Mansions*，杨宪益、戴乃迭译)

解 析

译文使用非谓语结构等表达方式,将原文具有同一主语"士隐"的分句进行整合,译为一个语义结构紧凑连贯的英语句子,使得译文结构紧凑合理,符合英语的语言表达特点和习惯。

例2-25

中文原文

第八十五条 营利法人的权力机构、执行机构作出决议的会议召集程序、表决方式违反法律、行政法规、法人章程,或者决议内容违反法人章程的,营利法人的出资人可以请求人民法院撤销该决议。但是,营利法人依据该决议与善意相对人形成的民事法律关系不受影响。

(《中华人民共和国民法典》)

英语译文

Article 85

A capital contributor of a for-profit legal person may request the people's court to revoke a resolution which is made at a meeting of the governing body or executive body of the legal person if the procedure for convening the meeting or the voting method thereof is in violation of the laws, administrative regulations, or the legal person's articles of association, or, if the content of the resolution violates the articles of association, provided that any civil juristic relationship already formed between the legal person and a bona fide third person based on such a resolution shall not be affected.

(*Civil Code of the People's Republic of China*)

解 析

译文使用连词等衔接方法,将原文两个涉及相同话题"营利法人"的汉语句子整合为一个结构复杂的英语句子,使得译文结构紧凑、语义连贯,符合法律文本的文体特点。

2. 在指示或指代处整合

汉语中经常会出现带有"这是"或"这个"等指示或指代成分的句子。在汉译英时,通常可以将具有指示意义或者具有指代作用的汉语句子与前一句进行整合,译为一个英语复杂句,以使译文结构紧凑连贯,符合英语的语言表达习惯。

例2-26

中文原文

核心价值观是文化软实力的灵魂、文化软实力建设的重点。这是决定文化性质和方向的最深层次要素。

（《习近平谈治国理政》）

英语译文

Core values, a fundamental factor for the texture and orientation of a culture, are the soul of cultural soft power and a key to building a nation's cultural soft power.

(*The Governance of China*)

解析

译文将具有指代作用的句子"这是决定文化性质和方向的最深层次要素"与前一句进行整合，使结构紧凑、语义连贯，符合英语的句式特点和语言表达习惯。

例2-27

中文原文

旧历新年快来了。这是一年中的第一件大事。除了那些负债过多的人以外，大家都热烈欢迎这个佳节的到来。

（《家》，巴金）

英语译文

The traditional New Year Holiday was fast approaching, the first event of the year, and everyone, except those who owed heavy debts — which traditionally had to be paid off before the end of the year — was enthusiastically looking forward to it.

(*The Family*, Sidney Shapiro 译)

解析

原文第二个句子中的"这"和第三个句子中的"这个佳节"都指代第一个句子中的"旧历新年"。译者对三个句子进行整合，将其译为一个英语复杂句，避免语义重复，符合英语的语言表达习惯。

例2-28

中文原文

　　干部有了丰富的基层经历，就能更好树立群众观点，知道国情，知道人民需要什么，在实践中不断积累各方面经验和专业知识，增强工作能力和才干。这是做好工作的基本条件。

（《习近平谈治国理政》）

英语译文

　　Extensive experience gained from working at local levels can help officials develop a sound attitude towards the people, know what the country is really like and what the people really need, be better versed in various jobs and professions, and become more competent and effective for meeting future requirements for good work performance.

(*The Governance of China*)

> **解 析**
>
> 　　译文将带有指代表达的句子"这是做好工作的基本条件"与前一句进行整合，使得译文结构紧凑、语义连贯，符合英语的句式特点和语言表达习惯。

3. 在语义逻辑关联处或连贯处整合

　　汉语并列短句之间通常存在隐含的逻辑关系（因果、假设、目的、方式等）。汉译英实践中，需要在语义逻辑关联处进行整合，整合时要注意通过逻辑关联词等将这些逻辑关系表示出来。此外，在语义连贯处也可以进行整合，如果汉语原文各短句包含的语义信息之间有清晰一致的脉络，可以根据意群对原句进行调整，将其整合成一个完整的句子或段落。

例2-29

中文原文

　　两年下来，知青已经能独立放牛放羊，可是狩猎还一窍不通。然而，在内蒙中东部边境草原的游牧生产方式中，狩猎好像占有更重要的位置。

（《狼图腾》，姜戎）

英语译文

　　In their two years on the grassland, they had learned to tend cows and sheep by themselves, but they were incompetent hunters, and in the nomadic existence of people in eastern Inner Mongolia, hunting ranks higher than tending livestock.

(Wolf Totem, Howard Goldblatt 译)

> **| 解　析**
>
> 　　译文根据原文的意群,在语义逻辑关联处进行整合,将具有转折和并列语义的句子整合为一个英语复合句,使得译文语义逻辑清晰、结构紧凑连贯。

| 例 2-30

中文原文

　　巴雅尔急忙改用两只手死死抓住了狼的一条后腿,死命后拽,一下子减弱了狼的前冲力。母子两人总算把狼拽停了步。

(《狼图腾》,姜戎)

英语译文

　　Bayar let go of the tail and grabbed one of the hind legs, pulling it backward and slowing the animal's forward progress until the two of them managed to stop it altogether.

(Wolf Totem, Howard Goldblatt 译)

> **| 解　析**
>
> 　　原文两个句子的话题都与"拽狼"相关。译者将两个在语义上具有连贯性的句子整合,使得译文语义更加连贯,符合英语的语言表达习惯。

| 例 2-31

中文原文

　　在农村长大的姑娘谁还不知道拣麦穗这回事。

　　我要说的,却是几十年前的那段往事。

　　或许可以这样说,拣麦穗的时节,也是最能引动姑娘们幻想的时节。

　　在那月残星稀的清晨,挎着一个空篮子,顺着田埂上的小路走去拣麦穗的时候,她想的是什么呢?

　　等到田野上腾起一层薄雾,月亮,像是偷偷地睡过一觉又悄悄地回到天边,她方才挎着装满麦穗的篮子,走回自家那孔窑的时候,她想的是什么呢?

　　唉,她还能想什么!

　　<u>假如你没有在那种日子里生活过</u>,你永远也无法想象,从这一颗颗丢在地里的麦穗上,会生出什么样的幻想。

(《拣麦穗》,张洁,选自《嬉雪:中国当代女性散文选(汉英对照本)》)

英语译文

　　What country girl wouldn't know about gathering wheat stalks! <u>Let me tell you</u> a story of long long ago <u>when you might almost say</u> that wheat gathering time was when girls' imaginations were the most alive.

　　In the early hours of dawn, under a waning moon and a sprinkling of stars, what would a girl with a basket on her arm be thinking of as she walked along the ridges in the fields on her way to gather wheat stalks? <u>When a thin mist hovered over the fields</u> and the moon rose silently again as if it had wakened from a stolen nap, what was the thinking of as she walked back home with a basket on her arm filled with wheat stalks? <u>Well</u>, what else could she think of? <u>If you had never been part of that life</u>, you will never know the dreams these stalks of wheat scattered in the fields could conjure up.

(*Gathering Wheat*,朱虹译,选自《嬉雪:中国当代女性散文选(汉英对照本)》)

┃ 解　析

　　译者将原文中语义关系较为紧密的段落进行整合,将原文六个段落译为两个英语语段,使得译文结构紧凑连贯。其中,将原文前三段整合为一段,聚焦背景叙述;将后三段整合为一段,聚焦拣麦穗的具体情景。

┃ 例2-32

中文原文

　　说完,站起来,做出宽怀大量的样子,一瘸一瘸走了,留下小林和小林老婆在那里发尴。

　　<u>由于有偷水这件事的介入</u>,使豆腐发馊事件变得不那么重要了。小林心里还责备老婆,一个大学生,什么时候学得这么市民气,偷了两桶水,值不了几分钱,丢人现眼让人数落了一顿。小林老婆也自感惭愧,就不好意思再追究馊豆腐一事,只是瞪了小林一眼,自己就下厨房做饭了。因为这件事的介入,使本来要爆发战争的家庭平静下来,小林又有些感激老头子。

(《一地鸡毛》,刘震云)

英语译文

Then he stands up, assumes a generous posture and limps away, leaving Young Lin and his wife feeling embarrassed. The intervention of this case makes the sour bean curd incident appear less important. Young Lin feels his wife is to blame. How could a university graduate become so vulgar? For two buckets of water which hardly costs anything, she has been disgraced by a sharp reproof. His wife feels quite ashamed herself and finds it difficult to go on complaining about the bean curd incident. Glancing at him angrily, she goes to the kitchen to prepare dinner. The incident has brought peace to his family just when it was on the brink of war. Young Lin is somewhat grateful to the old man for this.

(*Ground Covered with Chicken Feathers*, David Kwan 译)

解　析

原文第一段是对"偷水事件"经过的相关描述,第二段是对"偷水事件"之后发生的事情的叙述,两个段落之间存在叙事时间上的先后顺序以及语义上的连贯性。译者在语义连贯处进行整合,将原文的两个段落整合为一个段落,使得译文结构紧凑、语义连贯。

三、拆分与整合综合译法在汉译英中的应用

在实际的翻译实践中,拆分与整合作为一组相对应的翻译方法,并不总是独立使用的,通常会相互结合、相互补充,运用在汉译英翻译实践中。拆分与整合综合译法通常在以下情况运用。

1. 句子之内的拆分与整合

句子之内的拆分与整合指将一个汉语复句按照意群先进行拆分处理,然后再将拆分后的句子成分进行整合,译为符合英语句式结构要求和特点的英语句子。汉语的连动式施事句通常适用于此种译法。

例2-33

中文原文

贾珍吃过饭,盥漱毕,换了靴帽,命贾蓉捧着银子跟了来,回过贾母王夫人,又至这边回过贾赦邢夫人,方回家去,取出银子,命将口袋向宗祠大炉内焚了。

(《红楼梦》,曹雪芹)

英语译文

①After his meal, Jia Zhen washed and rinsed his mouth, then put on his boots and hat to go, accompanied by his son with the silver, to inform the Lady Dowager and Lady Wang and after them Jia She and Lady Xing that the bounty had been collected. This done, he returned home and took out the silver, ordering the bag to be burned in the large incense-burner in the Ancestral Temple.

(*A Dream of Red Mansions*, 杨宪益、戴乃迭译)

② After inspecting the yellow bag, Cousin Zhen had his lunch; then, when he had washed his hands and rinsed his mouth out, he changed into formal hat and boots and, ordering Jia Rong to follow him with the bag, set off for the other mansion to report the arrival of the bounty-money, first to Grandmother Jia and Lady Wang and then to Jia She and Lady Xing next door. When they got back he took out the money and ordered the bag to be carried into the Hall of the Ancestors and burnt there in the great incense-burner in front of the ancestral tablets.

(*The Story of the Stone*, David Hawkes 译)

解　析

原文为由多个动词结构组成的连动式施事句。杨宪益、戴乃迭和霍克斯的译文都在"方回家去"之前进行拆分，并根据英语句式表达需要，将拆分后的句子成分进行整合，译为两个英语复杂句，避免了译文过于冗长，使之符合英语的句式结构表达需要。

2. 句子之间的拆分与整合

句子之间的拆分与整合指将一个汉语复句中的分句进行拆分，并将其与相邻的另一个汉语句子或者其中的分句进行整合。

例2-34

中文原文

中国幅员辽阔，陆海兼备，地貌和气候复杂多样，孕育了丰富而又独特的生态系统、物种和遗传多样性，是世界上生物多样性最丰富的国家之一。中国的传统文化积淀了丰富的生物多样性智慧，"天人合一""道法自然""万物平等"等思想和理念体现了朴素的生物多样性保护意识。

(《中国的生物多样性保护》白皮书)

英语译文

China's land and sea territories are both vast; its complex terrain and diverse climate gave birth to unique ecosystems, abundant species, and rich genetic variety. As one of the most biodiverse countries in the world, China has a profound understanding of biodiversity, as manifest in traditional Chinese culture and these aphorisms: "Man is an integral part of nature"; "Dao follows the laws of nature"; and "All beings are equal".

(*Biodiversity Conservation in China*)

解 析

译文将原文第一句中的"是世界上生物多样性最丰富的国家之一"拆分出来,并与下一句中的"中国的传统文化积淀了丰富的生物多样性智慧"进行整合,译为"as one of the most biodiverse countries in the world, China has a profound understanding of biodiversity"。译者利用拆分与整合综合译法,使得译文结构更加紧凑、语义更加简洁连贯。

例2-35

中文原文

临回家时,老人作为牧场革委会委员,突然被留下开会,可是场部指示那些文件必须立即送往大队,不得延误。陈阵只好一人骑马回队。

(《狼图腾》,姜戎)

英语译文

Just before they were to head back, the old man was summoned to a meeting of the revolutionary committee. Since headquarters had said the study materials had to be delivered without delay, Chen was told to return alone.

(*Wolf Totem*, Howard Goldblatt 译)

解 析

译文在原文语义逻辑关联处进行拆分与整合翻译。在转折分句"可是场部指示……"前进行拆分,并与因果分句"陈阵只好一人骑马回队"进行整合,并使用连词"since",明晰地传达出原文的语义逻辑关系。

3. 不同语言层级的拆分与整合

不同语言层级的拆分与整合,指的是将汉语原文中的词、句和段等不同语言层级的语言成分同时进行拆分与整合翻译。在实际的翻译实践中,并非只在句子或者段落等某一个语言层级中使用拆分或整合译法,而是可以同时在不同语言层级中进行拆分与整合。例如,将汉语原文的一个段落拆分为若干个段落,同时将段落中的句子结构再进行拆分与整合。

┃ 例2-36

中文原文

蜀中山水,不知迷醉了多少古人和今人……

近年来,在四川北部南坪县境内,闪现出一颗五光十色的风光"宝石",这就是人们赞不绝口的"神话世界"九寨沟。它镶嵌在松潘、南坪、平武三县接壤的群山之中,面积约6万公顷,距成都约400公里。九寨沟,由树正群海沟、则查洼沟、日则沟三条主沟组成,海拔平均在2 500米左右。过去,沟中有九个藏族沟寨,因此得名。

(《神话世界九寨沟》,选自《散文佳作108篇》)

英语译文

Sichuan Province in southwest China is renowned for its many fascinating natural wonders which have attracted millions of travelers over the centuries. The recent discovery of the scenic beauty of Jiuzhaigou (Nine-village Ravine) has added charm to the picturesque landscape. Known as "China's Fairyland", Jiuzhaigou is located in the hills along the borders of Nanping, Pingwu and Songpan counties, some 400 kilometers from Chengdu, the provincial capital. Three scenic areas — Shuzheng qunhaigou, Zechawagou and Rizegou — combine to make up the 60,000 hectares of fairyland, which is nearly 2,500 meters above sea level. Its name "Nine-village Ravine" is supposed to be because Tibetans once inhabited nine villages in the ravine.

(*Jiuzhaigou, China's Fairyland*,何志范译,选自《散文佳作108篇》)

┃ 解 析

译者首先将原文的两个语段整合为一个段落,使得译文结构更加连贯紧凑;其次,译者将原文第二段第一句的最后一个分句"这就是人们赞不绝口的'神话世界'九寨沟"与下一句"它镶嵌在松潘、南坪、平武三县接壤的群山之中"进行整合,译为"known as 'China's Fairyland', Jiuzhaigou is located in the hills along the borders of Nanping, Pingwu and Songpan counties";此外,译者将原文中"面积约6万公顷"

从所在的句子中拆分出来,并与下一句中最后一个分句"海拔平均在2 500米左右"进行整合,译为"combine to make up the 60,000 hectares of fairyland, which is nearly 2,500 meters above sea level"。译文采用拆分与整合综合译法,简洁连贯,结构紧凑,更符合英语语言表达习惯和旅游文本的文体风格。

例2-37

中文原文

这幅三峡长卷的装帧也匠心独运。它采取中国传统的"折子"样式,启合自如,折叠起浑然一册,抖开来全幅在目。而其大小,恰似西方游客所喜爱的可以随手插在口袋里的Pocket Book。

画家说:"人家爱出大画册,我却欢喜这精美的袖珍长卷。它小巧玲珑,逗人喜爱,又携带方便,价廉物美。"艺术家的用心和中外旅游者购买旅游纪念品的心理需求是相通的。他尤其关注当今大多数旅游者的实际消费水平,小折子画卷比大型画册有更广阔的销售市场,从而让高雅的艺术走进芸芸寻常百姓之中。

(《三峡多奇景 妙笔夺天工》,选自《散文佳作108篇》)

英语译文

The highly decorative binding of the scroll is done in an accordion-like traditional paper-folding technique. When folded, it is a book; unfolded, the entire scene can be viewed. The book is pocket-size and very portable for western tourists. The painter says, "Many artists like to publish coffee-table books, I prefer the beauty, originality and portability of a small, long and elegant scroll at a reasonable price." Special attention has been paid to current consumer trends in tourism. The artist's intention corresponds with both Chinese and foreign tourists' preference in buying souvenirs. This folding "pocket scroll" has more appeal than a coffee-table book. Thus, beautiful and lofty art is made available to the general public.

(*The Scenic Three Gorges Captured in Their Essence*,

李海瑞译,选自《散文佳作108篇》)

解析

首先,译者将原文两个段落整合为一个语段,使得译文连贯紧凑;其次,译者将原文第一和第二个句子进行拆分与整合处理,将"这幅三峡长卷的装帧也匠心独运"和"它采取中国传统的'折子'样式"进行整合,译为"The highly decorative binding of the scroll is done in an accordion-like traditional paper-folding technique.",并将"启合自如,折叠起浑然一册,抖开来全幅在目"进行拆分,单独译为结构对称清晰的英语句子"When folded, it is a book; unfolded, the entire scene can be viewed."。此外,译者将原文中"我却欢喜这精美的袖珍长卷"和"它小巧玲珑,逗人喜爱,又携带方便,价廉物美"两个句子进行整合,译为"I prefer the beauty, originality and portability of a small, long and elegant scroll at a reasonable price.",使得译文简洁流畅,更符合英语的语言表达特点和习惯。

综上所述,拆分和整合是两种相对应的翻译方法,目的是使英语译文的结构衔接更加紧凑连贯,避免出现结构过于松散或者语义重复的英语译文。在汉译英翻译实践中,对于是否采用拆分译法、整合译法或者拆分与整合综合译法,以及在何种情况下进行拆分、整合翻译,可以根据汉语原文的语义信息分布、句法结构以及标点符号的使用、语段结构、文本效果和风格等因素进行分析,灵活使用同时,还可以考虑对汉语原文中的句子和段落等不同语言层级进行拆分和整合处理,综合使用拆分与整合译法。

练习题

1. 译文补充

下列句子摘自英语专业八级考试真题,请根据原文语义将以下译文补充完整,注意拆分与整合译法的运用。

(1)城市驱散了旷野原有的居民,破坏了旷野古老的风景,<u>越来越多地以井然有序的繁华,取代我行我素的自然风光</u>。

Cities have dispersed the indigenous inhabitants of the wilderness, destroyed the ancient landscape of the wilderness, _____

_____.

(2)今天,旷野日益退缩着,<u>但人们不应忽略旷野,漠视旷野,而要寻觅出与其相守的最佳间隙</u>。善待旷野就是善待人类自身。<u>要知道</u>,人类永远不可能以城市战胜旷野。

Nowadays, the wilderness is shrinking day by day. _____

_____.

To be kind to the wilderness is to be kind to human beings themselves. _____

_____ that human beings can never defeat the wilderness

with the city.

（3）中国传统文化犹如一条奔腾了五千年永不干涸的大河，她亦旧亦新，不断吐故纳新，
持续创新。

Chinese traditional culture is like a river that _____

_____.

She includes both old and new, constantly rejuvenating and innovating.

（4）你的青春就是一场远行，一场离自己的童年，离自己的少年，越来越远的远行。你会
发现这个世界跟你想象的一点都不一样，你甚至会觉得很孤独，你会受到很多的排
挤。度假和旅行，其实都解决不了这些问题，我解决问题的办法，就是不停寻找自己
所热爱的一切。

Youth is a journey into the distance, a journey that _____

_____. In this journey, you will find the world drastically different from what you

have imagined. _____.

In fact, neither going on a vacation nor taking a trip can solve these problems. _____

_____.

2. 句子翻译

将下列句子译为英语，注意拆分与整合译法的运用。

（1）中国式现代化，是中国共产党领导的社会主义现代化，既有各国现代化的共同特征，
更有基于自己国情的中国特色。

_____

_____

_____

（2）发展是党执政兴国的第一要务。没有坚实的物质技术基础，就不可能全面建成社会
主义现代化强国。

_____

_____

_____

（3）中国高度重视海洋生态文明建设,正在持续加强海洋环境污染防治,保护海洋生物多
样性,实现海洋资源有序开发利用,同时也愿在这些领域深化与各国的合作,共同为
海洋的绿色发展作出应有贡献。

_____

_____

_____

（4）一个亭亭玉立的少女出现在门里边,洁白的皮肤,俊秀的脸庞,黑亮的眼睛,长长的睫
毛,正吃惊地看着她。

_____

_____

_____

（5）很多时候,有没有新面貌,有没有新气象,并不在于制定一打一打的新规划,喊出一个
一个的新口号,而在于结合新的实际,用新的思路、新的举措,脚踏实地把既定的科学目
标、好的工作蓝图变为现实。

_____

_____

_____

（6）同过去相比,我们今天学习的任务不是轻了,而是更重了。这是由我们面临的形势和
任务决定的。

_____

_____

_____

（7）但对这个问题的分析不应到此为止,我们还需要作深入一层的探讨。这是因为,在市
场上进行活动的是各个交易人,一个交易人就是一个资源投入主体。

_____

_____

_____

（8）在中国这样一个大国,真正把14亿多人民的意愿表达好、实现好并不容易,必须有坚

强有力的统一领导。

_____

_____

_____

3. 段落翻译

以下段落摘自《共建"一带一路":构建人类命运共同体的重大实践》白皮书,请将其翻译为英文,注意拆分与整合译法的运用。

公元前140年左右的中国汉代,张骞从长安出发,打通了东方通往西方的道路,完成了"凿空之旅"。中国唐宋元时期,陆上和海上丝绸之路共同发展,成为连接东西方的重要商道。15世纪初的明代,郑和七次远洋航海,促进了海上丝绸之路商贸往来。千百年来,古丝绸之路犹如川流不息的"大动脉",跨越尼罗河流域、底格里斯河和幼发拉底河流域、印度河和恒河流域、黄河和长江流域,跨越埃及文明、巴比伦文明、印度文明、中华文明的发祥地,跨越佛教、基督教、伊斯兰教信众的汇集地,跨越不同国度和肤色人民的聚集地,促进了亚欧大陆各国互联互通,推动了东西方文明交流互鉴,创造了地区大发展大繁荣,积淀了以和平合作、开放包容、互学互鉴、互利共赢为核心的丝路精神。

_____

_____

_____

_____

_____

_____

_____

_____

_____

第三章
虚化与实化

虚化与实化是两种相对应的翻译方法。虚化译法是指将原文的具体化表达抽象化，也就是在翻译过程中将原文中具体的或者形象性的词语、短语、习语等表达进行虚化处理，用抽象性或者概括性的单词、词组或者句子进行翻译。实化译法是指将原文的抽象化表达形象化或具体化，也就是在翻译过程中将原文中抽象性或者概括性的成分进行实化处理，用形象性或者具体的单词、词组、句子进行翻译，从而消除或者减少英汉语言与文化差异所造成的翻译障碍，增强原文的可译性和译文的可读性，使得译文忠实通顺，也使译文对译入语读者所产生的效果与原文对源语读者产生的效果相同。

刘宓庆（2019）对"虚"与"实"进行了解释："虚"指虚化、淡化、抽象化；"实"是"虚"的反面，即实化、强化、具体化。刘宓庆（2019：327）认为，虚实问题的实质是如何将语言的意义看成可以灵活运动（而不是凝滞、僵化）的实体，它可以向抽象化的方面运动（即虚化），也可以向具体化的方向运动（即实化），这种运动就叫作引申。

连淑能（1993）指出，与英语相比，汉语用词倾向于具体，常常以实的形式表达虚的概念，以具体的形象表达抽象的内容。这主要是因为汉语缺乏像英语那样的词缀虚化手段。汉语虽较缺乏抽象词语，但形象性的词语（如成语、谚语、歇后语等）和表达手段（如比喻）却相当丰富。汉语常常借助这些生动具体的词语和形象化的表达手段来表达抽象笼统的意义。许多形象性词语有很强的民族色彩或特定的文化涵义。汉译英实践中，这类词语往往难以进行对应翻译，因而不得不借助虚化手段或其他翻译方法，以此增强可译性。

由于英语和汉语在语言、思维和文化等方面存在较大差异，在汉英翻译实践中，使用虚化和实化翻译方法的目的是增强译文的逻辑性和可读性，有效传达原文语义信息，使得译文的语义忠实于原文、语句通顺、逻辑清晰连贯、语言符合英语语言的特点和表达习惯。本章将借助汉译英翻译实践中的经典案例，举例分析虚化译法和实化译法在汉译英中的应用。

一、虚化译法在汉译英中的应用

刘宓庆（1984：14）指出："翻译一定要摆好虚与实的关系：翻译不可不实，不实则不信；翻译又不可太实，太实则不达。翻译不仅应功于实，还应功于虚。以虚寓实，尤应以虚寓不达之实；以虚求信，尤应以虚补不足之信。"汉语经常用实的形式表达虚的概念，倾向于使用具体的形象表达抽象的内容。因此，在汉译英翻译实践中，为了译文的忠实与通顺，有必要将原文中表达具体意义或者表示具体形象的词语、短语或习语等进行虚化，从而增强原文的可译性和译文的可读性。通常,汉语中的习语、特殊形式的数字表达和对义聚合体表达等具体、形象的表达形式,以及形象性修辞表达,在翻译过程中常应用虚化译法进行处理。

1. 习语的虚化

汉语中的习语等形象性表达相当丰富。习语是语言的精华,通常包括成语、俗语、格言、歇后语、谚语、俚语、行话等,其表现形式言简意赅、形象生动。习语大多带有浓厚的民族色彩和特定的文化内涵,往往难以进行对应翻译,因而有必要应用虚化译法,以增强其可译性。

▎例 3-1

中文原文

　　有的怕得罪人,怕丢选票,搞无原则的<u>一团和气</u>,信奉多栽花、少栽刺的庸俗哲学,<u>各人自扫门前雪、不管他人瓦上霜</u>,<u>事不关己高高挂起</u>,满足于做得过且过的太平官;……这种不求有功、但求无过的"圆滑官""老好人""推拉门""墙头草"多了,党和人民事业还怎么向前发展啊?

(《习近平谈治国理政》)

英语译文

　　Some officials <u>keep on good terms with everybody</u> at the expense of principles, for they are afraid of offending people and losing votes, holding a belief in the vulgar philosophy of "more flowers and fewer thorns." <u>They mind nothing but their own business and will do nothing unless their personal interests are affected</u>, being satisfied with muddling along and accomplishing nothing at all. ... How can the cause of the Party and the people proceed if there are a lot of "nice guys," people of "smooth character," those who always "pass the buck to others," or those who waver like "weeds atop the wall"?

(The Governance of China)

▎解　析

　　原文中"各人自扫门前雪、不管他人瓦上霜,事不关己高高挂起"等习语结构对称、言简意赅、形象生动,但是直译会使得译文冗长繁复、难以理解,影响可读性。译文应用虚化译法,将原文中的习语译为"they mind nothing but their own business and will do nothing unless their personal interests are affected"等,从而增加了译文的逻辑性和可读性,使得译文忠实通顺、简洁明晰。

例3-2

中文原文

回首百年，无论<u>风云变幻、沧海桑田</u>，中国青年爱党、爱国、爱人民的<u>赤诚追求</u>始终未改，坚定不移听党话、跟党走的<u>忠贞初心</u>始终未变。

（《新时代的中国青年》白皮书）

英语译文

Looking back on a century of <u>relentless change</u>, China's youth have never wavered in their <u>determination</u> to love the Party, the country and the people, nor in their <u>commitment to the original aspiration</u> of following the instructions and guidance of the Party.

(*Youth of China in the New Era*)

> **解 析**
>
> 译文应用虚化译法，将原文中"风云变幻、沧海桑田""赤诚追求""忠贞初心"等形象性的四字词语进行抽象化或概括化处理，分别译为"relentless change""determination"和"commitment to the original aspiration"，使得译文简洁流畅、忠实通顺，可读性增强。

例3-3

中文原文

铁匠<u>十有八九</u>性子急，老李却是慢性子，一根耙钉，也得打上两个时辰。但慢工出细活，这把耙钉，就打得<u>有棱有角</u>。

（《一句顶一万句》，刘震云）

英语译文

Most blacksmiths <u>tend to be</u> impatient men, but not Li. It took him up to four hours to hammer out a rake tine, but his slow, methodical work produced wares that were <u>second to none</u>.

(*Someone to Talk to*, Howard Goldblatt & Sylvia Li-chun Lin 译)

> **解 析**
>
> 译者应用虚化译法，根据语境将原文中两个形象具体的习语"十有八九"和"有棱有角"分别译为"tend to be"和"second to none"，使得译文简洁明晰、忠实通顺。

例3-4

中文原文

然后，我便从母亲的房间出来。我的脚鬼使神差地朝禾寡妇的房间走去。

（《私人生活》，陈染）

英语译文

Eventually I left her apartment, to have my feet carry me directly to Widow Ho's.

（*A Private Life*, John Howard-Gibbon 译）

解　析

译者采用虚化译法，并未直译原文中的成语"鬼使神差"，而是译为"my feet carry me directly to"，使得译文简洁、通顺、忠实。另外，译文中，由于"母亲"在前文已经出现过了，故此处用代词"her"译出。

例3-5

中文原文

老马是个赶大车的，你是个卖豆腐的，你们井水不犯河水，当年人家不拿你当人，你为啥非巴结他做朋友？有啥说法不？

（《一句顶一万句》，刘震云）

英语译文

Old Ma drove a cart, you sold *tofu*, so there was no need to have anything to do with one another. Why in the world did you do everything you could to make him like you when he refused to treat you as a friend?

（*Someone to Talk to*, Howard Goldblatt & Sylvia Li-chun Lin 译）

解　析

译者应用虚化译法，对原文中生动形象的习语"井水不犯河水"进行虚化处理，译为"there was no need to have anything to do with one another"；同时，"不拿你当人"这一通俗而形象的说法被虚化为了"refused to treat you as a friend"。

例3-6

中文原文

偏值近年水旱不收，<u>鼠盗蜂起</u>，无非抢田夺地，<u>鼠窃狗偷</u>，民不安生，因此官兵剿捕，难以安身。

（《红楼梦》，曹雪芹）

英语译文

① But the last few year's harvests had been ruined by flood and drought and <u>the countryside was overrun by bandits who seized fields and land</u>, giving the people no peace. The punitive expeditions by government troops only made matters worse.

(The Story of the Stone, David Hawkes 译)

② But a series of crop failures due to flooding and drought had led to <u>widespread brigandage in those parts</u>, and government troops were out everywhere hunting down the mutinous peasants and making arrests.

(A Dream of Red Mansions, 杨宪益、戴乃迭译)

> **解　析**
>
> 霍克斯和杨宪益、戴乃迭的译文均采用虚化译法，将原文中生动形象的四字成语"鼠盗蜂起"和"鼠窃狗偷"进行虚化处理，分别和"无非抢田夺地"结合起来，译为"the countryside was overrun by bandits who seized fields and land"和"widespread brigandage in those parts"，使得译文简洁明了、忠实通顺。

2. 数字表达的虚化

汉语中有许多用于虚指的特殊的数字表达形式，并非表示实际的数量，例如"七上八下""十有八九""一目十行"等，这些数字通常并无实义，只具有泛指意义或引申意义，主要用于传情达意或者增强语言的形象性和艺术性等。数字虚指广泛用于成语、俗语、歇后语等习语中。翻译时应运用虚化译法，用表示泛指意义的概括性词语或表示引申意义的抽象性词语进行表达。

例3-7

中文原文

党的十八大精神，说<u>一千道一万</u>，归结为一点，就是坚持和发展中国特色社会主义。

（《习近平谈治国理政》）

英语译文

The guiding principles of the Party's 18th National Congress, in essence, boil down to upholding and developing socialism with Chinese characteristics.

(*The Governance of China*)

解　析

　　原文中的习语"说一千道一万"并无实际的数字上的含义,只具有泛指意义或引申意义。译文采用虚化译法,将其译为"in essence",从而翻译出了其引申意义,使得译文忠实通顺。

例3-8

中文原文

　　此方人家多用竹篱木壁者,大抵也因劫数,于是接二连三,牵五挂四,将一条街烧得如火焰山一般。

(《红楼梦》,曹雪芹)

英语译文

① Since most of the nearby buildings had bamboo walls and were probably doomed to destruction, the flames spread from house to house until the whole street was ablaze like a flaming mountain.

(*The Story of the Stone*, David Hawkes 译)

② And, since the houses in this area all had wooden walls and bamboo fences — though also, doubtless, because they were doomed to destruction anyway — the fire leaped from house to house until the whole street was blazing away like a regular Fiery Mountain.

(*A Dream of Red Mansions*,杨宪益、戴乃迭译)

解　析

　　原文中的成语"接二连三"和"牵五挂四"中,数字并无实指,主要用于增强语言表达的形象性和艺术性。译者应用虚化译法,分别将其译为"spread from house to house"和"leaped from house to house",翻译出了其引申含义,使得译文忠实通顺。

例3-9

中文原文

陈阵脱掉皮袍,杨克勉强地把手电、铁钎和书包递给他,并用陈阵那条近两丈长的蒙袍腰带拴住了他的双脚,又把自己的长腰带解下来连接在陈阵的腰带上。

(《狼图腾》,姜戎)

英语译文

After Chen took off his deel, Yang reluctantly handed him the flashlight, the spade, and his bag. He tied Chen's Mongol sash, which was several feet long, around Chen's foot, then tied his own sash to Chen's.

(*Wolf Totem*, Howard Goldblatt 译)

解 析

原文中的数量表达"近两丈长"并非指精确的数量,译文应用虚化译法,将其译为"several feet long",取得了与原文相同的效果。

例3-10

中文原文

玄德看其人:身长九尺,髯长二尺;面如重枣,唇若涂脂;丹凤眼,卧蚕眉,相貌堂堂,威风凛凛。

(《三国演义》,罗贯中)

英语译文

Xuande looked over the newcomer item by item and noted his huge frame, his long beard, his dark brown face and deep red lips. He had eyes like a phoenix and fine bushy eyebrows like silk worms. His whole appearance was dignified and awe-inspiring.

(*Romance of the Three Kingdoms*, Brewitt-Taylor 译)

解 析

此例中,原文描写的是关羽的外貌,"身长九尺,髯长二尺"并非指关羽实际的身高和髯长。根据我国古代的度量标准换算,"九尺"约为两米至三米,"二尺"约为五十至六十厘米,此处均用以虚指,强调关羽身材高大,夸大其魁梧的形象。译文采用虚化译法,译为"huge frame"和"long beard",有效传达了原文的语义信息,

> 增强了译文的可读性,同时避免了因直译数量表达"九尺"和"二尺"而造成译文繁冗。

3. 对义聚合体表达的虚化

由于现代汉语中双音节词特别是双音节合成词占多数,而语素则多是单音节的,所以现代汉语可以形成众多的对义聚合体。对义聚合体词语指由同一上义词的各个子项构成的词语。对义聚合体可以由两个子项构成,如"父母""兄弟"等;也可以由多个子项构成,如"绫罗绸缎""悲欢离合""柴米油盐酱醋茶"等(曾剑平,2006)。汉语对义聚合体词语通常表示泛指意义,在汉译英过程中需要应用虚化译法,使用抽象性或者概括性的上义词表达进行翻译。

┃ 例 3-11

中文原文

　　当此,则自欲将已往所赖天恩祖德,锦衣纨袴之时,饫甘餍肥之日,背父兄教育之恩,负师友规训之德,以至今日一技无成,半生潦倒之罪,编述一集,以告天下人。

(《红楼梦》,曹雪芹)

英语译文

　　I decided then to make known to all how I, though dressed in silks and delicately nurtured thanks to the Imperial favour and my ancestors' virtue, had nevertheless ignored the kindly guidance of my elders as well as the good advice of teachers and friends, with the result that I had wasted half my life and not acquired a single skill.

(A Dream of Red Mansions,杨宪益、戴乃迭译)

┃ 解 析

　　译文采用虚化译法,将原文中的对义聚合词"锦衣纨袴""饫甘餍肥"以及"父兄"进行虚化处理,分别译为"dressed in silks"和"delicately nurtured"以及"my elders",使得译文简洁通顺、忠实恰当。需要注意的是原文中"天恩祖德"和"师友"并非由同一上义词的各个子项构成的词语,因此译文没有采用虚化译法,而是将其分别译为"the Imperial favour and my ancestors' virtue"和"teachers and friends"。

┃ 例 3-12

中文原文

　　人生在世,谁也替不了谁;生儿育女,不是为了父母,是为了儿女自己,各人的路,让他们自己闯去吧!

（《穆斯林的葬礼》,霍达）

英语译文

In life no one can take the place of another. <u>Children come into the world</u> not for the <u>parents</u>' sake, but to live <u>their</u> own lives. Leave them alone; let them choose their own ways.

(*The Jade King: History of a Chinese Muslim Family*,关月华、钟良弼译)

解 析

译者采用虚化译法,将原文中的对义聚合体表达"生儿育女""父母"和"儿女"进行虚化处理,将"生儿育女"和"父母"分别译为"children come into the world"和"parents",并将"儿女"译为第三人称代词的复数形式,指代前面出现过的"children"。这样处理使得译文简洁通顺,避免了繁冗和重复表达。

4.形象性修辞表达的虚化

汉语行文中倾向于使用大量带有比喻、拟人或夸张等修辞手段的形象性表达,以增强语言的生动性、形象性和艺术性。由于英汉语言和文化的差异,这些表达常常会造成翻译障碍。为了译文的忠实与通顺,在汉译英过程中,有必要应用虚化译法,对原文中的形象性修辞表达进行虚化处理,使用抽象性或概括性的表达进行翻译。

例 3-13

中文原文

群众路线是我们党的生命线和根本工作路线,是我们党永葆青春活力和战斗力的重要<u>传家宝</u>。

（《习近平谈治国理政》）

英语译文

The mass line is the Party's lifeline and fundamental work principle. It is a <u>cherished tradition</u> that enables our Party to maintain its vitality and combat capability.

(*The Governance of China*)

解 析

译文采用虚化译法,将原文中带有比喻修辞的形象性表达"传家宝"进行抽象化处理,译为"cherished tradition",从而增强了译文的可读性。

例3-14

中文原文

我们一定要始终<u>与人民心心相印</u>、与人民同甘共苦、与人民团结奋斗,夙夜在公,勤勉工作,努力向历史、向人民交出<u>一份合格的答卷</u>。

(《习近平谈治国理政》)

英语译文

We must always <u>bear in mind what the people think</u> and share weal and woe with them, and we must work together with them diligently for the public good and <u>for the expectations of history and of the people</u>.

(The Governance of China)

解 析

译文采用虚化译法,将带有比喻修辞的形象性表达"交出一份合格的答卷"进行虚化处理,译为"for the expectations of";对于原文中另一个生动形象的表达"与人民心心相印",译者也将其虚化为"bear in mind what the people think"。经过这样的处理,译文在语义上忠实于原文的同时,结构也较为简洁。

例3-15

中文原文

我们要适应新形势下群众工作的新特点新要求,深入做好组织群众、宣传群众、教育群众、服务群众工作,虚心向群众学习,诚心接受群众监督,始终<u>植根人民</u>、造福人民,始终保持党同人民群众的<u>血肉联系</u>,始终与人民心连心、同呼吸、共命运。

(《习近平谈治国理政》)

英语译文

We must organize our people, communicate with them, educate them, serve them, learn from them, and subject ourselves to their oversight. We should always <u>be part of the people</u>, <u>work for their interests</u>, and <u>maintain close ties</u> and <u>share good and bad times with them</u>.

(The Governance of China)

> **解 析**
>
> 译文采用虚化译法,将原文中的形象性表达"植根人民、造福人民"译为"be part of the people, work for their interests";将带有比喻修辞的表达"血肉联系"译为"maintain close ties";将形象性表达"心连心、同呼吸、共命运"译为"share good and bad times with them"。这种虚化处理方法使得译文结构简洁明晰,语义忠实通顺。

例3-16

中文原文

形象地说,理想信念就是共产党人精神上的"钙",没有理想信念,理想信念不坚定,精神上就会"缺钙",就会得"软骨病"。

(《习近平谈治国理政》)

英语译文

Put figuratively, the ideals and convictions of Communists are the marrow of their faith. Without, or with weak ideals or convictions, they would be deprived of their marrow and suffer from "lack of backbone".

(*The Governance of China*)

> **解 析**
>
> 译文采用虚化译法,将原文中带有比喻修辞的形象性表达"精神上的'钙'""缺钙""软骨病"等译为"marrow of their faith""be deprived of their marrow""lack of backbone"。这种虚化处理方式不仅使得译文忠实通顺,还增强了其可接受性和可读性。

例3-17

中文原文

在造林的规划布局上,由过去的"遍地开花"方式,转向按流域、山系相对集中造林。

(《摆脱贫困》,习近平)

英语译文

Forestation planning should turn from haphazard planting to targeted planting concentrated around select catchment areas and mountain ranges.

(*Up and Out of Poverty*)

> **解　析**
>
> 　　译文采用虚化译法，将原文中的形象性表达"遍地开花"抽象化，译为
> "haphazard planting"，使得译文简洁明晰、语义忠实准确，也使得译文读者更容易理
> 解"'遍地开花'方式"的造林规划布局。

例3-18

中文原文

　　关键是要健全权力运行制约和监督体系，让人民监督权力，<u>让权力在阳光下运行，
把权力关进制度的笼子里</u>。

（《习近平谈治国理政》）

英语译文

　　The solution to the problem of corruption is to improve the system that checks and
oversees the exercise of power, grant oversight powers to the people, and <u>make the exercise
of power more transparent and institutionalized</u>.

(The Governance of China)

> **解　析**
>
> 　　译文采用虚化译法，对"让权力在阳光下运行，把权力关进制度的笼子里"进
> 行抽象化和概括化处理，译为"make the exercise of power more transparent and
> institutionalized"，将原文中的形象性表达"在阳光下"译为"more transparent"，将带
> 有比喻修辞的表达"制度的笼子"译为"institutionalized"，这种虚化处理使得译文
> 忠实通顺的同时，语义也更加清晰简明。

二、实化译法在汉译英中的应用

　　汉语中有些词语表达的表层意思是抽象的，或者是表示其所属的性质或特点的，通常语
义虚泛笼统、含义模糊不明，在翻译过程中有必要应用实化译法，对抽象性、模糊性或概念性
的表达进行实化处理，即用具体的、明确的或形象的表达进行翻译，使得译文语义明晰、易于
理解，从而增强译文的逻辑性和可读性，有效传达原文的语义信息。在汉译英实践中，汉语
原文中的虚泛冗余修饰成分、模糊主语以及抽象语义可以应用实化译法进行翻译。

1. 虚泛冗余修饰成分的实化

　　由于汉语双音节词语的语言特点以及修辞文体等表达形式的需要，汉语表达中存在

大量虚泛夸张的表达以及冗余重复的修饰成分。在汉译英时，可以应用实化译法，删繁就简、避虚就实，使用简洁明确、形象具体的表达进行翻译，从而使得译文语义明确、逻辑结构明晰。

例3-19

中文原文

　　在新民主主义革命时期，中国青年不怕牺牲、敢于斗争，经受了生与死的考验，为争取民族独立、人民解放冲锋陷阵、抛洒热血。在社会主义革命和建设时期，中国青年勇于拼搏、甘于奉献，经受了苦与乐的考验，在新中国的广阔天地忘我劳动、发愤图强。在改革开放和社会主义现代化建设新时期，中国青年开拓创新、勇立潮头，经受了得与失的考验，为推动中国大踏步赶上时代锐意改革、拼搏奋进。

（《新时代的中国青年》白皮书）

英语译文

During the New Democratic Revolution (1919–1949), they rose to the occasion without fear of death and fought bravely for national independence and the people's liberation. During the socialist revolution and reconstruction (1949–1978), they endured hardships and dedicated themselves to building the newly-founded country. In the new period of reform, opening up and socialist modernization, those with a talent for innovation who were open to challenges stood out and forged ahead, led reform, and ensured that China progressed with the times.

(Youth of China in the New Era)

解析

　　由于汉语双音节词语的语言特点以及修辞文体等表达形式的需要，原文中存在"不怕牺牲、敢于斗争""冲锋陷阵、抛洒热血""勇于拼搏、甘于奉献""忘我劳动、发愤图强""开拓创新、勇立潮头""锐意改革、拼搏奋进"以及"经受了生与死的考验""经受了苦与乐的考验""经受了得与失的考验"等意思相近或虚泛冗余的修饰成分，主要是为了增强语势以及语言的形象性和艺术性，符合汉语文体的表达特点。由于英汉语言的差异，译文采用实化译法，删繁就简、避虚就实，使用简洁明确、形象具体的表达概括性地译为"rose to the occasion without fear of death and fought bravely""endured hardships and dedicated themselves to building the newly-founded country"和"those with a talent for innovation who were open to challenges stood out and forged ahead"等形式，使得译文语义明确、逻辑结构明晰。

例 3-20

中文原文

我怀想着故乡的雷声和雨声。那隆隆的有力的搏击，从山谷返响到山谷，仿佛春之芽就从冻土里震动，惊醒，而怒苗出来。

（《雨前》，何其芳，选自《英译中国现代散文选（汉英对照）》）

英语译文

I can never forget the thunderstorm we often had in my hometown. Over there, whenever the rumble of thunder reverberated across the valley, the buds of spring would seem to sprout freely after being disturbed and roused up from their slumber in the frozen soil.

（*Praying for Rainfall*，张培基译，选自《英译中国现代散文选（汉英对照）》）

解　析

译者采用实化译法，将"那隆隆的有力的搏击，从山谷返响到山谷"和"震动，惊醒，而怒苗出来"这两个冗余虚泛的修饰成分译为"the rumble of thunder reverberated across the valley""being disturbed and roused up from their slumber"，使得译文简洁明晰、通顺流畅。

例 3-21

中文原文

小车在层峦叠嶂中穿行，两旁是密密层层的参天绿树：苍绿的是松柏，翠绿的是竹子，中间还有许许多多不知名的、色调深浅不同的绿树，衬以遍地的萋萋的芳草。

（《绿的歌》，冰心）

英语译文

The small car wound its way over hill and dale, both sides of the road thickly wooded with towering green foliage; pines, cypresses and emerald bamboo. And there were many other trees whose names I did not know. The varied green of the trees were set off by a luxuriant carpet of scented lawn.

（*Ode to Green*，Paul White 译）

解 析

> 译文采用实化译法,将原文"许许多多不知名的、色调深浅不同的绿树"中的虚泛冗余修饰词"许许多多不知名的"和"色调深浅不同的"进行拆分,并将"色调深浅不同的绿树"与后半句"衬以遍地的萋萋的芳草"进行合译,译为"The varied green of the trees were set off by a luxuriant carpet of scented lawn."这一完整的英语句子,避免了直接顺译"许许多多不知名的、色调深浅不同的"这一较长的修饰成分而造成译文冗长,使得译文更加简洁、清晰、连贯,更加符合英语的表达习惯。

2. 模糊主语的实化

由于汉语是注重意合的语言,不受主谓一致句法结构的限制,所以存在很多无主句或者主语不明晰的句子结构。然而,英语是注重形合的语言,受主谓一致句法结构的制约。因此,在汉译英实践中,应运用实化译法,使原文中虚化或者模糊不清的主语得以明确。

例 3-22

中文原文

　　未来五年,中国航天将紧紧抓住数字产业化、产业数字化发展机遇,面向经济社会发展和大众多样化需求,加大航天成果转化和技术转移,丰富应用场景,创新商业模式,推动空间应用与数字经济发展深度融合。拓展卫星遥感、卫星通信应用广度深度,实施北斗产业化工程,为国民经济各行业领域和大众消费提供更先进更经济的优质产品和便利服务。培育发展太空旅游、太空生物制药、空间碎片清除、空间试验服务等太空经济新业态,提升航天产业规模效益。

（《2021 中国的航天》白皮书）

英语译文

In the next five years, China's space industry will seize the opportunities presented by the expanding digital industry and the digital transformation of traditional industries, to promote the application and transfer of space technology. Through innovative business models and the deep integration of space application with digital economy, more efforts will be made to expand and extend the scope for applying satellite remote-sensing and satellite communications technologies, and realizing the industrialized operation of the BeiDou Navigation Satellite System. This will provide more advanced, economical, high-quality products and convenient services for all industries and sectors and for mass consumption. New business models for upscaling the space economy such as travel, biomedicine, debris removal and experiment services will be developed to expand the industry.

(China's Space Program: A 2021 Perspective)

| 解　析

　　由于汉语不受主谓一致句法结构的限制,原文中存在无主句结构或者主语不明晰的句子结构。然而,英语注重形合,受主谓一致句法结构的制约。因此,译文运用实化译法,分别用"China's space industry""more efforts"和"new business models for upscaling the space economy ..."作主语,使原文中虚化或模糊不清的主语在译文中得以明确。

| 例3-23

中文原文

　　金融科技监管框架初具雏形。发布实施云计算、个人金融信息保护、区块链安全、金融APP、应用程序编程接口等多项金融科技规则。研究包容审慎、富有弹性的创新试错容错机制,为金融科技创新划定刚性底线、设置柔性边界、预留充足发展空间,探索既能守住安全底线,又能鼓励合理创新的新型监管工具并在北京启动测试验证。金融科技产品纳入国推认证体系,持续强化金融科技质量管理,切实防范因技术产品缺陷引发的风险向金融领域传导。

(《中国人民银行2019年度报告》)

英语译文

　　The fintech regulatory framework took shape. The PBC released many fintech rules covering cloud computing, personal financial information protection, blockchain security, financial apps, and APIs. It studied the test-and-trial mechanism for innovation that is inclusive, prudent and flexible, and defined the fundamental requirements, boundaries and leeway of fintech innovation. It also explored novel regulatory instruments that can ensure security while encouraging innovation, and kick-started tests in Beijing. It pushed the incorporation of fintech products into the certification system uniformly promoted by the state, improved fintech quality management and prevented the spillover of risks arising from technical weaknesses to the financial sector.

(The People's Bank of China 2019 Annual Report)

| 解　析

　　译文采用实化译法,将原文中隐含的主语"the PBC"译出,并使用了多个"it"作主语,指代"the PBC",使得译文逻辑清晰、语义明确。

例 3-24

中文原文

立足新发展阶段,贯彻新发展理念,构建新发展格局,推动高质量发展,将使大陆综合实力和国际影响力持续提升,大陆对台湾社会的影响力、吸引力不断扩大,我们解决台湾问题的基础更雄厚、能力更强大,必将有力推动祖国统一进程。

(《台湾问题与新时代中国统一事业》白皮书)

英语译文

Grounding its effort in the new development stage, the mainland is committed to applying the new development philosophy, creating a new development dynamic, and promoting high-quality development. As a result, the overall strength and international influence of the mainland will continue to increase, and its influence over and appeal to Taiwan society will keep growing. We will have a more solid foundation for resolving the Taiwan question and greater ability to do so. This will give a significant boost to national reunification.

(The Taiwan Question and China's Reunification in the New Era)

> **解 析**
>
> 译文采用实化译法,将原文中隐含的主语"the mainland"译出,并使用了代词"we"和"this"作主语,使得译文逻辑清晰、语义明确。

3. 抽象语义的实化

汉语虽然倾向于使用形象具体的表达,但是也存在大量抽象性或概括性的语义表达。对于这类表达,在汉译英实践中,可以应用实化译法,使用具体形象的词语或句子进行翻译,从而增强译文的可读性。

例 3-25

中文原文

坚持独立自主,就要坚定不移走中国特色社会主义道路,既不走封闭僵化的老路,也不走改旗易帜的邪路。

(《习近平谈治国理政》)

英语译文

Adhering to independence means that we will firmly take the socialist path with Chinese characteristics. We will not take <u>the old path of a rigid closed-door policy</u>, nor <u>an erroneous path by abandoning socialism</u>.

(The Governance of China)

> **| 解　析**
>
> 　　译文采用实化译法,将原文中的抽象性表达"封闭僵化的老路"和"改旗易帜的邪路"具体化,译为 "the old path of a rigid closed-door policy" 和 "an erroneous path by abandoning socialism",使得译文简洁明晰。

▎例 3-26

中文原文

　　小林在机关待了五六年,<u>机关那一套</u>还不熟悉?

(《一地鸡毛》,刘震云)

英语译文

　　Young Lin has been in the office for about six years so he knows <u>the ins and outs of the routines</u>.

(Ground Covered with Chicken Feathers, David Kwan 译)

> **| 解　析**
>
> 　　原文中出现了抽象隐含性表达"机关那一套"。译文采用实化译法,进行具体化处理,将其译为 "the ins and outs of the routines",从而使得译文形象生动,产生与原文同样的效果。

▎例 3-27

中文原文

　　他们大意了。<u>大意之中过了元旦</u>;元旦之前,别的家长都<u>向阿姨们送东西</u>,或多或少,<u>意思意思</u>,惟独小林家<u>没有意思</u>,于是迹象就出现在孩子身上。

(《一地鸡毛》,刘震云)

英语译文

　　They have been <u>negligent about</u> the New Year. All the other children's parents <u>gave gifts</u>, big or small, to the nursery teachers, except them, and their child has suffered the consequences.

(Ground Covered with Chicken Feathers, David Kwan 译)

| 解　析

　　译文采用实化译法，将原文中带有抽象隐含性意义的表达"向阿姨们送东西，或多或少，意思意思"进行形象化处理，译为"gave gifts, big or small, to the nursery teachers"，从而增强了译文的可读性和译入语读者的可接受性。此外，译者将原文中"他们大意了。大意之中过了元旦"译为"They have been negligent about the New Year."，将两个"大意"合译为"negligent about"，阐明了原文的语义，同时避免了译文重复，使之简洁明晰。

| 例3-28

中文原文

　　宣传思想工作一定要把围绕中心、服务大局作为基本职责，胸怀大局、把握大势、着眼大事，找准工作切入点和着力点，做到因势而谋、应势而动、顺势而为。

（《习近平谈治国理政》）

英语译文

Our publicity and theoretical work must help us accomplish the central task of economic development and serve the overall interests of the country. Therefore, we must bear the big picture in mind and keep in line with the trends. We should map out plans with focus on priorities and carry them out in accordance with the situation.

(The Governance of China)

| 解　析

　　译文采用实化译法，将原文中"围绕中心、服务大局"等抽象概括性表达具体化，译为"accomplish the central task of economic development and serve the overall interests of the country"；同时，将"胸怀大局、把握大势、着眼大事""因势而谋、应势而动、顺势而为"等为了达到增强语势的效果而使用的虚泛冗余修饰成分译为"bear the big picture in mind and keep in line with the trends""in accordance with the situation"。这样处理后，得到的译文语言简洁明晰，可读性强。

| 例3-29

中文原文

　　阮小二道："如今该管官司没甚分晓，一片糊涂！千万犯了迷天大罪的倒都没事！我弟兄们不能快活；若是但有肯带挈我们的，也去了罢！"

（《水浒传》，施耐庵）

英语译文

"The authorities can't do anything about it. They're stupid block-heads," said Second. "Thousands of men who've committed towering crimes are wandering around free as air! We brothers are unhappy with our lot. We'd leave here gladly if we could find someone to lead us."

(*The Outlaws of the Marsh*, Sidney Shapiro 译)

> **解 析**
>
> 译者采用实化译法,将原文中的"没甚分晓""一片糊涂""迷天大罪""倒都没事"以及"不能快活"等抽象的表达分别译为"can't do anything about it""they're stupid block-heads""towering crimes""wandering around free as air"以及"unhappy with our lot"等具体形象的表达,使得译文忠实通顺、可读性增强。

总体而言,英语语言倾向于使用抽象概念表达具体的事物,比较注重抽象思维的运用;汉语语言倾向于使用形象具体的事物表达抽象的概念,比较注重形象思维的运用。但是,抽象与具体只是相对而言的,英语中存在大量具体或形象性的表达,汉语中也不乏抽象性或概括性的表达。因此,在翻译过程中有必要对汉语原文中的形象性表达进行虚化处理,从而翻译出其深层含义;或者对汉语原文中的抽象性表达进行实化翻译,从而增强译文的可读性,使得译文忠实通顺。在汉译英翻译实践中,应根据具体情况灵活应用虚化和实化译法。

练习题

1.译文补充

下列句子摘自党的二十大报告,请根据原文语义将以下译文补充完整,注意虚化与实化译法的运用。

(1)腐败是危害党的生命力和战斗力的最大毒瘤,反腐败是最彻底的自我革命。

Corruption is _____ to _____
_____ and _____
_____ of the Party, and fighting corruption is the most thorough kind of self-reform there is.

(2)坚持理论武装同常态化长效化开展党史学习教育相结合,引导党员、干部不断学史明理、学史增信、学史崇德、学史力行,传承红色基因,赓续红色血脉。

We will combine theoretical study with _____

study of the Party's history and see that Party members and officials strengthen their understanding, conviction, integrity, and diligence through continued study of Party history and _____.

(3) 时代呼唤着我们,人民期待着我们,唯有<u>矢志不渝、笃行不怠</u>,方能<u>不负时代、不负人民</u>。

_____, and the people expect us to deliver.

Only by _____ will we be able to

_____.

(4) 这是我们在长期实践中得出的至关紧要的规律性认识,必须倍加珍惜、始终坚持,<u>咬定青山不放松</u>,引领和保障<u>中国特色社会主义</u>巍巍巨轮乘风破浪、行稳致远。

It is a conclusion of paramount importance that we must cherish, uphold, and _____

_____. Under its guidance, we will ensure that

_____.

(5) 构建人类命运共同体是世界各国人民前途所在。<u>万物并育而不相害,道并行而不相悖</u>。只有各国行天下之大道,和睦相处、合作共赢,繁荣才能持久,安全才有保障。

Building a human community with a shared future is the way forward for all the world's peoples. An ancient Chinese philosopher observed that "_____

_____." Only when all countries

_____, live in harmony, and engage

in cooperation for mutual benefit will there be sustained prosperity and guaranteed security.

2. 句子翻译

将下列各句中文译为英文,注意虚化与实化译法的运用。

(1) 当然,实践是不断发展的,我们的认识和工作也要与时俱进,看准了的要及时调整和完善,但不要换一届领导就兜底翻,更不要为了显示所谓政绩去另搞一套,不要空洞的新口号满天飞。

_____

_____

_____

（2）对干部应实行"任期目标责任制"，以便加以考核。干部"只上不下"，当然不对。干部"能上能下"的提法，也不一定妥当。应该是干部"有上有下"，该上就上，该下就下。应该是：干部当得好的就上，当不好就下。在干部任免上，没有照顾的问题。

_____

_____

_____

（3）要树立正确政绩观，多做打基础、利长远的事，不搞脱离实际的盲目攀比，不搞劳民伤财的"形象工程""政绩工程"，求真务实，真抓实干，勇于担当，真正做到对历史和人民负责。

_____

_____

_____

（4）1949 年 10 月 1 日，中华人民共和国成立，中国人民从此站立起来、当家做主，真正成为新国家新社会的主人。面对一穷二白、百业凋敝的困难局面，中国共产党团结带领人民自力更生、艰苦奋斗，发奋图强、重整山河。

_____

_____

_____

（5）实践锻炼不是去"镀金"，更不是去走过场等着提拔，如果那样，必然会身子去了心没去，还是与群众格格不入，那就是弄虚作假了。

_____

_____

_____

（6）我们要坚持对马克思主义的坚定信仰、对中国特色社会主义的坚定信念，坚定道路自信、理论自信、制度自信、文化自信，以更加积极的历史担当和创造精神为发展马克思主义作出新的贡献，既不能刻舟求剑、封闭僵化，也不能照抄照搬、食洋不化。

_____

_____

_____

(7) 对于国际事务,中国始终从中国和世界人民的根本利益出发,根据事情本身的是非曲直,决定自己的立场政策。从不依附谁,也不胁迫谁;不惹事,也不怕事。无论国际形势多么复杂严峻,外来压力如何霸凌蛮横,我们都不信邪、不弯腰,始终用自己的脑袋思考,用自己的双脚走路,把中国的命运牢牢掌握在自己手中。

_____

_____

_____

(8) 那只猫咪被领来时就已经很大,光滑而肥硕,它的适应力之强悍令我惊诧,它见食就吃,见窝就睡,见人就摇尾讨好,有奶就是娘,结果它一直活着,没有像我那只固执别扭的麻雀的命运。这使我终生痛恨猫这一种偷生苟活的宠物,它们在我眼中是一群毫无气节的投机主义者,正像我长大后所见到过的其他类别的嘴脸一样。

_____

_____

_____

(9) 按说,凭咱们的交情,过去小小不言的来往,都不用签字画押的,可这一回,我也是舍着老本儿啊,不怕一万,就怕万一,空口无凭,还是立约为证,亲兄弟,明算账,先小人,后君子,日后钱货两清,大家都圆满,啊?

_____

_____

_____

3. 段落翻译

以下段落摘自第三十四届韩素音国际翻译大赛竞赛原文,请将其翻译为英文,注意虚化与实化译法的运用。

　　非遗"活"起来、"火"起来,正是推动传统文化创造性转化、创新性发展的生动映照。"非遗进校园""非遗进景区""非遗购物节"等活动广泛开展;文旅部在国家级贫困县设立的非遗扶贫就业工坊,成为帮助群众增收致富的"金钥匙";在一些地方,非遗保护被写入村规民约,助力乡村振兴……越来越多的非遗从田野巷陌中"走出来",传承与发展的生命力就蕴藏在人们的看见、了解与热爱中。这些启示我们,让非遗"见人见物见生活",才能更好促进经济社会发展,不断惠益人民福祉。

第四章

省略与增补

　　省略与增补是两种相对应的翻译方法。省略译法主要包括语言上的省略和内容上的省略，其中汉译英中的语言省略主要指省略修饰语、省略范畴名词、省略动词、省略重复以及省略修辞性成分等；内容省略主要为省略原文中不适宜译入目标语的内容。增补译法也包括语言增补和内容增补两个方面。汉译英实践中常见的语言增补主要指译文中代词、连词和冠词的添加；内容增补主要指文化背景知识的增补和逻辑成分的增补。

一、省略译法在汉译英中的应用

　　一般而言，汉译英中的省略有两种情况，一是语言省略，二是内容省略。

1. 语言省略

　　语言省略是指为了适应目标语（本书中主要指英语）行文简洁、清晰的特征，同时也为了更准确地传达出原文的表达意图，从语法和修辞两个角度考虑，把原文中一些词减去不译。语言省略也被称为减译法，遵循的基本原则是"减词不减意"。因此，这种省略法指的不是漏译，而是使英译文洗练的主要路径。在我国译者中，杨绛是这方面的典范，她称这种方法为"点烦"。许多人往往会主观地认为，省略译法是翻译中一种较为简单的方法。实则不然，"点烦"是在更高的层面对译文语言进行的提升，也就是通常所说的"译审"的工作。在《失败的经验（试谈翻译）》一文中，杨绛（1986）详细阐述了"点烦"的内涵及两个注意事项：

　　　　简掉可简的字，就是唐代刘知几《史通》《外篇》所谓"点烦"。芟芜去杂，可减掉大批"废字"，把译文洗练得明快流畅。这是一道很细致、也很艰巨的工序。一方面得设法把一句话提炼得简洁而贴切，一方面得留神不删掉不可省的字。在这道工序里得注意两件事。（一）"点烦"的过程里不免又颠倒些短句。属于原文上一句的部分，和属于原文下一句的部分，不能颠倒，也不能连结为一句，因为这样容易走失原文的语气。（二）不能因为追求译文的利索而忽略原文的风格。如果去掉的字过多，读来会觉得迫促，失去原文的从容和缓。如果可省的字保留过多，又会影响原文的明快。这都需译者掌握得宜。我自己就掌握不稳，往往一下子去掉了过多的字，到再版的时候又斟酌添补。

　　为了说明这一方法，杨绛（1986）还举了下面的短例：

译文(一):他们都到某处去了。我没有和他们同到那里去,因为我头晕。

译文(二):他们都到某处去了。我头晕,没去。

两个译文相比较,一目了然,译文(二)较译文(一)更简洁,更洗练,更符合地道汉语的表达习惯。原因有两点:一是译文(二)通过颠倒语序的方式实现逻辑关系的表达。译文(一)中用连词"因为"表达出了第二句话中两个小句间的因果逻辑关系,但译文(二)通过将"我头晕"前置,就自然形成了和后面的"没去"之间的因果关系,因此完全可以省去因果连接词"因为"。二是译文(二)省去了代词。译文(一)中第二句话的第一个小句中有三个代词:"我""他们"和"那里"。实际上,除了"我"以外的两个代词,其内容在上一句中都已讲过,无需重复,因此完全可以省去。再者,汉语也不习惯过多地使用代词。

此外,翻译中存在迁移性冗余现象,对此也需要采用省略译法进行处理。翻译中的迁移性冗余指的是,并不按照译文语言的内在组合规律,而是将原文中的语言组合形式直接迁移到译文中,从而造成译文的冗余性表达,并影响译文的交流效果的现象。例如,在中文中我们可以说"我们必须厉行节约,减少不必要的开支"。实际上,这句话中前后两个小句讲的是一回事,即中文中的"一事两说"现象。在英语译文中,一般应只保留一个小句。如果直译为"We must practice economy and reduce unnecessary expenditures.",就会造成英语译文中存在迁移性冗余,影响译文的表达效果。英语文体权威专家普遍认为,英语文体贵在简洁。斯特伦克(Strunk,1979:23)在其著作《文体的要素》(The Element of Style)中指出,有力的文章是简洁的。一句话不应包含多余的词,一段话不应包含多余的句,正如一幅画不应包含多余的线条,一台机器不应包含多余的零件。这也就是说,在翻译实践中,我们应该把一句话中不起任何作用的词删掉。

对于汉译英中的省略,在外文出版社和中央编译局做过八年译文修改工作的翻译专家平卡姆(Pinkham,2000)称之为"去除冗余"。平卡姆(2000)曾一针见血地指出,词语冗余(unnecessary words)是中式英语的标志。也就是说,词语冗余是汉译英实践中一大棘手问题。平卡姆(2000)还指出,汉译英中的迁移性冗余主要有五大类:冗余的名词和动词(unnecessary nouns and verbs),冗余的修饰语(unnecessary modifiers),冗余的成对词(redundant twins),一事两说(saying the same thing twice),重复指称(repeated references to the same thing)。

整体来看,汉译英中,语言省略主要包括以下五个方面。

(1)省略修饰语

程镇球(1980)指出,从事汉译英笔头工作时常会碰到一个棘手问题,那就是如何在译文里处理好原文中的修饰词。这里讲的修饰词指的是修饰名词的形容词或词组和修饰动词、形容词的副词或词组。汉语中修饰语较多,尤其在中文政治文献中,为了加强语气,通常使用较多修饰语,特别是副词性修饰语。当然,英语中也用修饰语,但相对来说英语中的修饰语要少得多。在汉语中,修饰语用得越多,表示强调的程度越高,但在英语中往往恰恰相反。

例 4-1

中文原文

中国将坚定不移走生态优先、绿色低碳的高质量发展道路，坚持不懈推动绿色低碳发展。

（《中国关键词：生态文明篇》）

英语译文

China will prioritize eco-environmental conservation and pursue green, low-carbon and high-quality development.

(*Keywords to Understand China: On Eco-civilization*)

解析

在此例中，中文原文中的"坚定不移""坚持不懈"两个副词性修饰词都没有译出。在英语中，"will"已表示比较强的语气。如果不是特别强调"坚定不移"和"坚持不懈"，仅用"will"表达足矣。

例 4-2

中文原文

各地区各部门要切实担负起稳定经济的责任，积极推出有利于经济稳定的政策。

（《2022年政府工作报告》）

英语译文

All localities and government departments should fulfill their responsibilities for maintaining stable macroeconomic performance by proactively introducing pro-stability policies.

(*Report on the Work of the Government, 2022*)

解析

在此例中，原文中的副词"切实"修饰动词"担负起"，起到加强语气的作用，译文采用省略译法，省略了副词性修饰语"切实"，将"切实担负起"译为"fulfill"，表达出了相同的含义。

（2）省略范畴名词

中文中的范畴名词较多，如：形势、水平、工作、问题、领域、情况、做法、事业、局面等。

这些范畴名词实际上无实质内容，因此在英译时一般可省略。例如，"经济领域的改革"可译为"reforms in the economy"或"economic reforms"，而不是"reforms in the sphere of the economy"。

例4-3

中文原文

强化稳岗扩就业政策落实，扎实做好高校毕业生等重点群体就业工作，推进大众创业万众创新。

（《2022年政府工作报告》）

英语译文

We intensified policies to stabilize and expand employment, took solid measures to ensure employment for key groups like college graduates, and encouraged business startups and innovation.

(*Report on the Work of the Government, 2022*)

解析

在此例中，"就业"后的范畴名词"工作"没必要翻译，因此译者略去了"工作"一词，将"就业工作"译为"employment"。

例4-4

中文原文

发展社会主义先进文化，提高社会文明程度，弘扬诚信文化，建设诚信社会，提升公共文化服务水平，健全现代文化产业体系。

（《2021年政府工作报告》）

英语译文

We will develop advanced socialist culture, raise standards of public civility, promote integrity and trustworthiness throughout society, improve public cultural services, and improve modern systems for cultural industries.

(*Report on the Work of the Government, 2021*)

解析

在此例中，"水平"作为范畴名词，无实质意义，没必要译出。

例4-5

中文原文

坚持对外开放的基本国策,着力实现合作共赢,开放型经济水平显著提升。

（《2018年政府工作报告》）

英语译文

... with a commitment to China's fundamental policy of opening up, we have focused on promoting win-win cooperation, and significantly improved the performance of our country's open economy.

(*Report on the Work of the Government, 2018*)

解 析

有些范畴词虽无实意,但也可以翻译为具有实际意义的表达。在此例中,译者未将范畴词"水平"省略,而是将其译为了"performance",具体表达了原文中"水平"的隐含含义。

例4-6

中文原文

大力发展科技、教育事业,培养高素质的人才队伍,是国家强盛、民族复兴的必由之路。

（《2012年政府工作报告》）

英语译文

To make China prosperous and strong and achieve the revival of the Chinese nation, we need to vigorously develop science, technology, and education and create a high-quality talent pool.

(*Report on the Work of the Government, 2012*)

解 析

在此例中,"事业"为范畴名词,因此将"教育事业"译为"education"即可。

例4-7

中文原文

这里需要注意的一个问题是:物价稳定、提供较多就业机会、提高劳动者实际收入这三方面的情况是有所不同的。

(《中国经济改革发展之路》,厉以宁)

英语译文

What merits attention in this regard is that investment impacts price stability, the creation of jobs, and labor income in different ways.

(*Economic Reform and Development the Chinese Way*,凌原译)

解　析

　　译文采用省略译法,对原文中的范畴词"问题""机会"和"情况"进行省略处理,使得译文简洁明晰、忠实通顺、可读性强。

例4-8

中文原文

　　如果经济确实处于瓦尔拉均衡状态,那么市场在资源配置中的自我制约作用将是明显的。

(《中国经济改革发展之路》,厉以宁)

英语译文

If an economy is exactly in Walrasian equilibrium, the market will be highly self-restraining in resource allocation.

(*Economic Reform and Development the Chinese Way*,凌原译)

解　析

　　译文采用省略译法,将原文中的范畴词"均衡状态"译为"equilibrium",使得译文简洁通顺。

(3) 省略动词

　　整体来说,汉语的动态性强,英语的静态性强。因此,在语言成分的使用方面体现为汉语用动词较多,而英语用名词较多。英语中名词的使用还与文体的正式程度有关,文体越正式,名词的使用就越多,如政治文献、法律法规等。

例4-9

中文原文

　　进入21世纪以来,气候变化、冰川融化、塑料污染、电子垃圾激增等环境问题日益突出，让我们不得不重新思考人类与自然的关系。

（《华为投资控股有限公司2020年可持续发展报告》）

英语译文

The 21st century has seen a sharp increase in the severity of climate change, melting glaciers, plastic pollution, soaring e-waste, and other environmental problems, forcing us to reassess our relationship with nature.

(Huawei Investment & Holding Co., Ltd. 2020 Sustainability Report)

解　析

> 在中文原文中，有一系列八个动词，但在英语译文中只有一个谓语动词 "has seen"。

很明显，汉语中动词用得多，英语中名词用得多。一方面，这是英语的文体要求；另一方面，这也是由于英语中的动词有屈折变化，使用起来不够方便，而汉语中的动词没有屈折变化，可作各种句法成分，使用起来较为方便。即使在翻译文学文本时，这种动词省略或弱化的现象也同样存在。

例 4-10

中文原文

心中想着，忽见丫鬟话未报完，已进来了一位年轻的公子：头上戴着束发嵌宝紫金冠，齐眉勒着二龙抢珠金抹额；穿一件二色金百蝶穿花大红箭袖，束着五彩丝攒花结长穗宫绦，外罩石青起花八团倭锻排穗褂；登着青缎粉底小朝靴。

（《红楼梦》，曹雪芹）

英语译文

① Daiyu was wondering what sort of graceless scamp or little dunce Baoyu was and feeling reluctant to meet such a stupid creature when, even as the maid announced him, in he walked. He had on a golden coronet studded with jewels and a golden chaplet in the form of two dragons fighting for a pearl. His red archer's jacket, embroidered with golden butterflies and flowers, was tied with a colored tasseled palace sash. Over his he wore a turquoise fringed coat of Japanese satin with a raised pattern of flowers in eight bunches. His court boots were of black satin with white soles.

(A Dream of Red Mansions，杨宪益、戴乃迭译)

② "I wonder," thought Dai-yu, "just what sort of graceless creature this Bao-yu is going to be!" The young gentleman who entered in answer to her unspoken question had a small jewel-encrusted gold coronet on the top of his head and a golden headband low down over his brow in the form of two dragons playing with a large pearl.

He was wearing a narrow-sleeved, full-skirted robe of dark red material with a pattern of flowers and butterflies in two shades of gold. It was confined at the waist with a court girdle of coloured silks braided at regular intervals into elaborate clusters of knotwork and terminating in long tassels.

Over the upper part of his robe he wore a jacket of slate-blue Japanese silk damask with a raised pattern of eight large medallions on the front and with tasselled borders.

On his feet he had half-length dress boots of black satin with thick white soles.

(*The Story of the Stone*, David Hawkes 译)

③ He was, in fact, a young man of tender years, wearing on his head, to hold his hair together, a cap of gold of purplish tinge, inlaid with precious gems. Parallel with his eyebrows was attached a circlet, embroidered with gold, and representing two dragons snatching a pearl. He wore an archery-sleeved deep red jacket, with hundreds of butterflies worked in gold of two different shades, interspersed with flowers; and was girded with a sash of variegated silk, with clusters of designs, to which was attached long tassels; a kind of sash worn in the palace. Over all, he had a slate-blue fringed coat of Japanese brocaded satin, with eight bunches of flowers in relief; and wore a pair of light blue satin white-soled, half-dress court shoes.

(*The Dream of the Red Chamber*, H. Bencraft Joly 译)

┃ 解　析

　　我们看到,在中文原文中,用了六个具体的描写穿着的状态动词:"戴着""勒着""穿""束着""外罩""登着",可谓是每一件服饰都用了不同的表示穿戴的动词。但在杨宪益和戴乃迭、霍克斯、乔利(H. Bencraft Joly)三者的译文中,动词基本用的是两个:"have"和"wear"。乔利的译文稍微多了些变化,还用了"was attached"和"was girded with"。整体来说,三则英译文中都出现了省略或弱化动词的现象。

（4）省略重复

汉译英中,要省略的重复有两种,一是显性的重复,二是隐性的重复。显性的重复,指表面就能看到的重复,如:

┃ 例4-11

中文原文

　　再一个是有些人担心干预。不能笼统地担心干预,有些干预是必要的。要看这些干预是有利于<u>香港人</u>的<u>利益</u>，<u>有利于</u><u>香港的繁荣和稳定</u>，还是<u>损害</u><u>香港人</u>的<u>利益</u>，<u>损害</u><u>香港的繁荣和稳定</u>。

（《邓小平文选》）

英语译文

Other people are afraid of intervention. Again, we should not fear all interventions; intervention in some cases may be necessary. The question is whether it <u>is good or bad for</u> <u>the interests of the people of Hong Kong</u> and for <u>prosperity and stability there</u>.

(Selected Works of Deng Xiaoping)

│ 解 析

　　这是邓小平同志1984年10月3日会见港澳台同胞国庆观礼团时谈话的内容。在此句中，"香港人的利益"与"香港的繁荣和稳定"各重复了两遍。如果在英语译文中保留这种重复，译文就会显得拖沓。因此，译者巧妙地将"有利于"和"损害"整合在一起，译为"is good or bad for"，后面就可以共享宾语"the interests of the people of Hong Kong"和"prosperity and stability there"。这样不仅去掉了原文中的重复，还将"香港的繁荣和稳定"中的"香港"转换为了代词"there"，使译文读来非常简练。

│ 例 4-12

中文原文

父亲和罗汉大爷披着蓑衣，坐在罩子灯旁，听着<u>河水的低沉呜咽——非常低沉的呜咽</u>。

（《红高粱》，莫言）

英语译文

Father and Uncle Arhat, rain capes over their shoulders, sat around the shaded lamp listening to <u>the low gurgling of the river</u>.

(Red Sorghum，Howard Goldblatt 译)

│ 解 析

　　为了起到强调的文学表达效果，原文中重复表达了"低沉的呜咽"之意，属于显性重复表达。译文省略了重复的内容"非常低沉的呜咽"，将"河水的低沉呜咽——非常低沉的呜咽"译为"the low gurgling of the river"。

隐性的重复，则要进行英汉语的比对才能识别，处理难度大于显性重复，如：

例 4-13

中文原文

科技创新，就像撬动地球的杠杆，总能创造<u>令人意想不到的奇迹</u>。当代科技发展历程充分证明了这个过程。

（《习近平谈治国理政》）

英语译文

Scientific and technological innovations, like a fulcrum which is said to be able to lever the earth, always create <u>miracles</u>. This has been proved in the development of contemporary science and technology.

(The Governance of China)

解 析

原文中的"奇迹"一词已包含"令人意想不到的"之意。译文采用省略译法，省略了原文中的隐性重复内容"令人意想不到的"，将"令人意想不到的奇迹"直接译为"miracles"。

例 4-14

中文原文

……夺取新时代中国特色社会主义<u>伟大</u>胜利，为实现中华民族<u>伟大复兴</u>的中国梦不懈奋斗。

（《习近平谈治国理政》）

英语译文

... strive for the <u>great success</u> of socialism with Chinese characteristics for a new era, and work tirelessly to realize the Chinese Dream of national <u>rejuvenation</u>.

(The Governance of China)

解 析

在此例中，中文原文有两个"伟大"，但英语译文只翻译了第一个；第二个"伟大"也就是"复兴"前的"伟大"并没有翻译，而是省去了。这是因为，在英语中"rejuvenation"本身就是一个意义重大的词，在其前面再添加修饰语"great"，就有夸张之嫌。

（5）省略修辞性成分

汉语讲究文采，较多使用夸张、隐喻等修辞手法。英语讲究语言平实，其中较少含有夸张、隐喻等修辞性成分。汉译英中,若省略掉这些修辞性成分时不影响对原文语义的传达,这些修辞性成分就可以省略。特别是,当修辞性成分译入英语后可能引起英语读者的困惑、不解与误解时,这些成分通常应进行省略处理。

例4-15

中文原文

把握经济运行合理区间的上下限,抓住发展中的突出矛盾和结构性问题,定向施策,聚焦靶心,精准发力。

(《2015年政府工作报告》)

英语译文

With a keen understanding of the appropriate range within which the economy needs to be operating, we adopted targeted steps to address the serious issues and structural problems hindering development.

(*Report on the Work of the Government, 2015*)

> **解 析**
>
> 中文原文将解决矛盾隐喻性地比作了一个射箭的过程:先定向,再瞄准,最后发射,是一个事件隐喻。《2015年政府工作报告》英译本省略性地翻译出了其中实质性的部分 "adopted targeted steps",因射箭这个隐喻很少在英语中用来描述政府的工作方法或工作过程,可能会引起英语读者的不解。

例4-16

中文原文

要增强斗争精神,敢于亮剑、敢于斗争,坚决防止和克服嗅不出敌情、分不清是非、辨不明方向的政治麻痹症。

英语译文

We need to build up our fighting spirit, take an unequivocal stance, and resolutely prevent and overcome political lethargy, which will render us unable to detect hostile moves, distinguish right from wrong, or see the correct direction.

(本例来自黄友义讲座"学深悟透、精准翻译、有效传播
——参加党政文献翻译的体会",苏州大学,2021年11月17日)

> **解 析**
>
> 　　在中文的语境下，我们经常使用军事隐喻来描述日常工作，但这在英语语境下较为少见。因此，"敢于亮剑、敢于斗争"没有直接翻译，而是省略性地翻译其实质内容，译为"take an unequivocal stance"。

例 4-17

中文原文

　　对目前遇到的困难，有的民营企业家形容为遇到了"三座大山"：市场的冰山、融资的高山、转型的火山。

（《习近平谈治国理政》）

英语译文

Mired in the current predicament, some entrepreneurs have identified three stumbling blocks — an underheated market, financing hurdles, and business model transformation woes.

(The Governance of China)

> **解 析**
>
> 　　中文原文将民营企业遇到的困难隐喻性地形容为了"三座大山"，但在英译文中省略了修辞表达，直接译为了"three stumbling blocks"。同时，译文也省略了原文中"冰山""高山"和"火山"的修辞性表达，并对其具体含义进行了阐释，将"市场的冰山、融资的高山、转型的火山"译为了"an underheated market, financing hurdles, and business model transformation woes"。

例 4-18

中文原文

　　山峦层林尽染，平原蓝绿交融，城乡鸟语花香。这样的自然美景，既带给人们美的享受，也是人类走向未来的依托。无序开发、粗暴掠夺，人类定会遭到大自然的无情报复；合理利用、友好保护，人类必将获得大自然的慷慨回报。我们要维持地球生态整体平衡，让子孙后代既能享有丰富的物质财富，又能遥望星空、看见青山、闻到花香。

（《习近平谈治国理政》）

英语译文

Lush mountains, vast tracts of forest, blue skies, green fields, singing birds, and blossoming flowers offer more than visual beauty. They are the basis for our future development. Nature punishes those who exploit and plunder it brutally, and rewards those who use and protect it carefully. We must maintain the overall balance of the Earth's ecosystems, not only to ensure that future generations can continue to access material wealth, but also to protect their right to enjoy <u>the wonders of the natural world</u>.

(The Governance of China)

| 解　析

中文原文中的"山峦层林尽染，平原蓝绿交融，城乡鸟语花香""又能遥望星空、看见青山、闻到花香"采用了形象性的修辞手法，译者对此都进行了省略翻译，未保留原文中的所有形象。

2. 内容省略

从文化层面上来讲，原文中的有些内容不适宜译入目标语中。如果将这些内容译入目标语文本，就有可能引起不适或文化冲突。因此，作为文化间的协调者（mediator）或守门人（gatekeeper），译者应对这些内容进行过滤，进而在译文中省略，以便使翻译文本能够被目标语受众所接受。这就是内容省略。

当然，省译一定要把握好度，过度的省译就是漏译，从而会造成翻译中文化信息传播的失真。《西游记》一开头就铺垫了我国古代文化中宇宙产生的故事，即盘古开天辟地的故事，并交代了故事发生的东方背景。对于这些有关中国文化的重要元素，不同译者采取了不同的态度和不同的处理方式。

| 例4-19

中文原文

感盘古开辟，三皇治世，五帝定伦，世界之间，遂分为四大部洲：曰东胜神洲，曰西牛贺洲，曰南赡部洲，曰北俱芦洲。这部书单表东胜神洲。海外有一国土，名曰傲来国。国近大海，海中有一座山，唤为花果山。此山乃十洲之祖脉，三岛之来龙，自开清浊而立，鸿蒙判后而成。真个好山！有词赋为证。赋曰：

势镇汪洋，威宁瑶海。势镇汪洋，潮涌银山鱼入穴；威宁瑶海，波翻雪浪蜃离渊。木火方隅高积上，东海之处耸崇巅。丹崖怪石，削壁奇峰。丹崖上，彩凤双鸣；削壁前，麒麟独卧。峰头时听锦鸡鸣，石窟每观龙出入。林中有寿鹿仙狐，树上有灵禽玄鹤。瑶草奇花不谢，青松翠柏长春。仙桃常结果，修竹每留云。一条涧壑藤萝密，四面原堤草色新。正是百川会处擎天柱，万劫无移大地根。

那座山，正当顶上，有一块仙石。其石有三丈六尺五寸高，有二丈四尺围圆。三丈六尺五寸高，按周天三百六十五度；二丈四尺围圆，按政历二十四气。上有九窍八孔，按九宫八卦。四面更无树木遮阴，左右倒有芝兰相衬。盖自开辟以来，每受天真地秀，日精月华，感之既久，遂有灵通之意。内育仙胞，一日迸裂，产一石卵，似圆球样大。因见风，化作一个石猴，五官俱备，四肢皆全。便就学爬学走，拜了四方。目运两道金光，射冲斗府。惊动高天上圣大慈仁者玉皇大天尊玄穹高上帝，驾座金阙云宫灵霄宝殿，聚集仙卿，见有金光焰焰，即命千里眼、顺风耳开南天门观看。二将果奉旨出门外，看的真，听的明。须臾回报道："臣奉旨观听金光之处，乃东胜神洲海东傲来小国之界，有一座花果山，山上有一仙石，石产一卵，见风化一石猴，在那里拜四方，眼运金光，射冲斗府。如今服饵水食，金光将潜息矣。"玉帝垂赐恩慈曰："下方之物，乃天地精华所生，不足为异。"

（《西游记》，吴承恩）

英语译文

① There was a rock that since the creation of the world had been worked upon by the pure essences of Heaven and the fine savours of Earth, the vigour of sunshine and the grace of moonlight, till at last it became magically pregnant and one day split open, giving birth to a stone egg, about as big as a playing ball. Fructified by the wind it developed into a stone monkey, complete with every organ and limb. ...

(*Monkey*, Arthur Waley 译)

② After Pan Gu created the universe, by separating earth and sky with his mighty ax, the world was divided into four continents, in the north, south, east, and west. Our story takes place in the east.

By a great ocean lay a land called Aolai, within which was a mountain called Flower-Fruit, home to sundry immortals. What a mountain it was: of crimson ridges and strange boulders, phoenixes and unicorns, evergreen grasses and immortal peaches. And on its peak sat a divine stone, thirty-six and a half feet high, twenty-four in circumference. Since creation, this rock had been nourished by heaven and earth, the sun and the moon, until it was divinely inspired with an immortal embryo, and one day gave birth to a stone egg, about as large as a ball. After exposure to the air, it turned into a stone monkey, with perfectly sculpted features and limbs. ...

(*Monkey King: Journey to the West*, Julia Lovell 译)

③ Following Pan Gu's construction of the universe, the rule of the Three Kings, and the ordering of the relations by the Five Emperors, the world was divided into four great continents. They were: the East Pūrvavideha Continent, the West Aparagodānīya Continent, the South Jamūbdvīpa Continent, and the North Uttarakuru Continent. This book is solely concerned with the East Pūrvavideha Continent.

Beyond the ocean there was a country named Aolai. It was near a great ocean, in the midst of which was located the famous Flower-Fruit Mountain. This mountain, which constituted the chief range of the Ten Islets and formed the origin of the Three Islands, came into being after the creation of the world. As a testimonial to its magnificence, there is the following poetic rhapsody:

> *Its majesty commands the wide ocean;*
>
> *Its splendor rules the jasper sea;*
>
> *Its majesty commands the wide ocean*
>
> *When, like silver mountains, the tide sweeps fishes into caves;*
>
> *Its splendor rules the jasper sea*
>
> *When snowlike billows send forth serpents from the deep.*
>
> *On the southwest side pile up tall plateaus;*
>
> *From the Eastern Sea arise soaring peaks.*
>
> *There are crimson ridges and portentous rocks,*
>
> *Precipitous cliffs and prodigious peaks.*
>
> *Atop the crimson ridges*
>
> *Phoenixes sing in pairs:*
>
> *Before precipitous cliffs*
>
> *The unicorn singly rests.*
>
> *At the summit is heard the cry of golden pheasants;*
>
> *In and out of stony caves are seen the strides of dragons:*
>
> *In the forest are long-lived deer and immortal foxes;*
>
> *On the trees are divine fowls and black cranes.*
>
> *Strange grass and flowers never wither:*
>
> *Green pines and cypresses always keep their spring.*
>
> *Immortal peaches are ever fruit-bearing;*
>
> *Lofty bamboos often detain the clouds.*
>
> *Within a single gorge the creeping vines are dense;*
>
> *The grass color of meadows all around is fresh.*
>
> *This is indeed the pillar of Heaven, where a hundred rivers meet-*
>
> *The Earth's great axis, in ten thousand kalpas unchanged.*

There was on top of that very mountain an immortal stone, which measured thirty-six feet and five inches in height and twenty-four feet in circumference. The height of thirty-six feet and five inches corresponded to the three hundred and sixty-five cyclical degrees, while the circumference of twenty-four feet corresponded to the twenty-four solar terms of the calendar.

On the stone were also nine perforations and eight holes, which corresponded to the Palaces of the Nine Constellations and the Eight Trigrams. Though it lacked the shade of trees on all sides, it was set off by epidendrums on the left and right. Since the creation of the world, it had been nourished for a long period by the seeds of Heaven and Earth and by the essences of the sun and the moon, until, quickened by divine inspiration, it became pregnant with a divine embryo. One day, it split open, giving birth to a stone egg about the size of a playing ball. Exposed to the wind, it was transformed into a stone monkey endowed with fully developed features and limbs. Having learned at once to climb and run, this monkey also bowed to the four quarters, while two beams of golden light flashed from his eyes to reach even the Palace of the Polestar. The light disturbed the Great Benevolent Sage of Heaven, the Celestial Jade Emperor of the Most Venerable Deva, who, attended by his divine ministers, was sitting in the Cloud Palace of the Golden Arches, in the Treasure Hall of the Divine Mists. Upon seeing the glimmer of the golden beams, he ordered Thousand-Mile Eye and Fair-Wind Ear to open the South Heaven Gate and to look out. At this command the two captains went out to the gate, and, having looked intently and listened clearly, they returned presently to report, "Your subjects, obeying your command to locate the beams, discovered that they came from the Flower-Fruit Mountain at the border of the small Aolai Country, which lies to the east of the East Pūrvavideha Continent. On this mountain is an immortal stone which has given birth to an egg. Exposed to the wind, it has been transformed into a monkey, who, when bowing to the four quarters, has flashed from his eyes those golden beams that reached the Palace of the Polestar. Now that he is taking some food and drink, the light is about to grow dim." With compassionate mercy the Jade Emperor declared, "These creatures from the world below are born of the essences of Heaven and Earth, and they need not surprise us."

(*The Journey to the West*, 余国藩译)

> **┃ 解 析**
>
> 对比三则译文，我们看到，对于原文中有关中国文化的重要元素，韦利（Arthur Waley）不以为然，在其英译文中全部略去了，可谓是漏译；蓝诗玲（Julia Lovell）在其译文中，对于我国古代神话传说中盘古开天辟地的传说，在一定程度上进行了保留；而美籍华裔学者余国藩不仅对《西游记》原文中盘古开天辟地的神话传说故事进行了全译，同时也对中间的一首词进行了全译。

二、增补译法在汉译英中的应用

汉译英中的增补也包括两个方面：一是语言增补；二是内容增补。

1. 语言增补

语言增补,指的是由于汉语中较少使用代词、连词和冠词,因此译入英语时需要添加相应的代词、连词和冠词。这是英语语言系统本身的要求。

(1)代词的增补

例4-20

中文原文

不忘初心,方得始终。中国共产党人的初心和使命,就是为中国人民谋幸福,为中华民族谋复兴。这个初心和使命是激励中国共产党人不断前进的根本动力。全党同志一定要永远与人民同呼吸、共命运、心连心,永远把人民对美好生活的向往作为奋斗目标,以永不懈怠的精神状态和一往无前的奋斗姿态,继续朝着实现中华民族伟大复兴的宏伟目标奋勇前进。

(《习近平谈治国理政》)

英语译文

Never forget why you started, and you can accomplish your mission. The original aspiration and mission of Chinese Communists is to seek happiness for the Chinese people and rejuvenation for the Chinese nation. This original aspiration, this mission, is what inspires Chinese Communists to advance. In our Party, each and every one of us must always breathe the same air as the people, share the same future, and stay truly connected to them. The aspirations of the people to live a better life must always be the focus of our efforts. We must keep on striving with endless energy towards the great goal of national rejuvenation.

(*The Governance of China*)

| 解 析

这是习近平总书记在中国共产党第十九次全国代表大会上的报告中的内容。我们看到,中文原文中没有使用一个代词,但英译文中添加了七个代词。

例4-21

中文原文

上德不德,是以有德;下德不失德,是以无德。

(《道德经》)

英语译文

The man of highest "power" does not reveal himself as a possessor of "power";

Therefore he keeps his "power".

The man of inferior "power" cannot rid it of the appearance of "power";

Therefore he is in truth without "power".

(*Tao Te Ching*, Arthur Waley 译)

解　析

　　这是《道德经》第三十八章中的一句话。这句话的意思是：具备上德的人，不自以为有"德"，因任自然，其"德"不表现为形式上的"德"，所以是真正的"有德"；具备下德的人则恪守形式上的"德"（不失德即形式上不离开"德"），所以是真正的"无德"。韦利在英译文中添加了多个中文中没有的名词和代词。

汉译英实践中，是否增补代词取决于译者对语境的解读。对于一则文本，有时不同的译者会有不同的解读，因此添加的代词也会有所不同。

┃例4-22

中文原文

生查子·元夕

欧阳修

去年元夜时，花市灯如昼。

月上柳梢头，人约黄昏后。

今年元夜时，月与灯依旧。

不见去年人，泪湿春衫袖。

英语译文

① **At The New Year Lantern Festival**

Last year the first month's moon was full.

Like day the flower-fair lanterns shone.

The moon climbed to the willow tops.

I trysted her at yellow dusk.

This year the first month's moon is full.

The moon and lanterns are the same.

I cannot see her anywhere.

My Spring robe sleeves are wet with tears.

(The Herald Wind, Clara M. Candlin 译)

② **Sheng Ch'a Tzu**

Last year the night of the first full moon-

Flower-market lanterns bright as day-

The moon climbed high into the willow

As after dark, we met

This year, night and time the same

Moon and lanterns are as bright

But where is last year's you?

Tears stain spring, wet my sleeve.

(Beyond Spring, Julie Landau 译)

| 解　析

　　两个英译文相比,我们看到译文①将中文原文中隐藏的一对恋人间的关系解读为"I"和"her"的关系,是一种外叙事视角,读者的体验感不强。译文②则将这对恋人间的关系解读为"I"和"you"的关系,是一种内叙事视角,读者读来有强烈的体验感。

(2) 连词的增补

| 例4-23

中文原文

　　开放伤害不了我们。我们的同志就是怕引来坏的东西,最担心的是会不会变成资本主义。恐怕我们有些老同志有这个担心。搞了一辈子社会主义、共产主义,忽然钻出个资本主义来,这个受不了,怕。影响不了的,影响不了的。肯定会带来一些消极因素,要意识到这一点,但不难克服,有办法克服。

(《邓小平文选》)

英语译文

Opening will not hurt us. Some of our comrades are always worried that if we open up, undesirable things may be brought into China. <u>Above all</u>, they worry that the country might go capitalist. I'm afraid some of our veteran comrades do harbour such misgivings. <u>Since</u> they have been devoted to socialism and communism all their lives, they are horrified by the sudden appearance of capitalism. They can't stand it. <u>But</u> it will have no effect on socialism. No effect. Of course, some negative elements will come in, <u>and</u> we must be aware of that. <u>But</u> it will not be difficult for us to overcome them; we'll find ways of doing so.

(Selected Works of Deng Xiaoping)

| 解 析

　　汉语是意合的语言,通常不直接使用逻辑连接词以体现句子间的逻辑关系。我们看到,中文原文没有使用连词。但英译文中增加了"if""since""but""and"等连词,还增补了副词词组"above all"。译者对句子间的顺序和结构进行调整,重新梳理和明示原文的逻辑关系。

| 例4-24

中文原文

　　网络化、数字化、个性化、终身化已成为信息时代教育发展的重要特征,华为通过云、AI、5G等技术能力,并联合生态的力量,<u>让更多人平等地获取知识和技能,释放自身潜能,为社会创造更多价值</u>。

(《华为投资控股有限公司2020年可持续发展报告》)

英语译文

　　Networked, digital, personalized, and lifelong learning are key features of education today. Huawei will continue to harness cloud, AI, and 5G, and to work with our ecosystem partners to give more people equal access to knowledge and skills, <u>so that</u> they can unleash their potential and create more value for society.

(Huawei Investment & Holding Co., Ltd. 2020 Sustainability Report)

| 解 析

　　在中文原文中,"让更多人平等地获取知识和技能""释放自身潜能""为社会创造更多价值"是三个并列的小句。但在英语译文中,译者添加了连词"so that",明示了原文中没有直接显现出来的逻辑关系。

例4-25

中文原文

道之以政,齐之以刑,民免而无耻。道之以德,齐之以礼,有耻且格。

(《论语》)

英语译文

If the people be led by laws, and uniformity sought to be given them by punishments, they will try to avoid the punishment, but have no sense of shame.

If they be led by virtue, and uniformity sought to be given them by the rule of propriety, they will have the sense of shame, and moreover will become good.

(*The Confucian Analects*, James Legge 译)

解 析

《论语》中这句话的意思是:用法制禁令去引导百姓,使用刑法来约束他们,老百姓只是求得免于犯罪受惩,却失去了廉耻之心;用道德教化引导百姓,使用礼制去统一百姓的言行,百姓不仅会有羞耻之心,而且也会从心里归服。理雅各(James Legge)在翻译时,添加了连词"if"和"but",明示了原文中的条件关系。此外,还添加了副词性的连接词"moreover"。

(3) 冠词的增补

例4-26

中文原文

韧性城市

即具备在逆变环境中承受、适应和快速恢复能力的城市,是城市安全发展的新范式。主要指城市在面临自然和社会压力冲击,特别是遭受重大安全事故、极端天气、地震、洪涝、重大疫情等突发事件时,能够凭借其动态平衡、冗余缓冲和自我修复等特性,保持抗压、存续、适应和可持续发展的能力。北京市《关于加快推进韧性城市建设的指导意见》,围绕城市空间韧性、工程韧性、管理韧性和社会韧性,对韧性城市建设进行了顶层设计。

英语译文

A resilient city

This is a city that has an ability to withstand, adapt to and recover quickly from an adverse or changing environment. They represent a new paradigm for urban growth in a safe environment.

A city is resilient in the sense that it has built up a cushion against unexpected shocks, and it can reorient itself depending on the circumstances when a natural disaster or a major accident occurs, especially in the event of major safety accidents, extreme weather, earthquakes, floods, major epidemics and other emergencies. As a result, it is able to deal with the pressure, adapt, survive, and quickly return to the path of sustainable development. In its "Guidelines on Building a Resilient City", the municipal government laid down a master plan for building up the city's resilience in areas including urban space planning, construction, urban management and society.

（本例中文原文和英语译文均来自中国公共政策翻译研究院
公众号发布的文章"首都关键词"）

| 解　析

　　汉语中没有冠词这个词类，因此在汉译英中要特别注意冠词的增补。通过对比，我们可以清楚地看到，英语译文中添加了众多定冠词和不定冠词。另外，由于本例原文节选自"首都关键词"一文，因此第三句中的"北京市"没有直接译出，而是用"the city"等表达来指代。

| 例4-27

中文原文

　　红海早过了。船在印度洋面上开驶着。但是太阳依然不饶人地迟落早起，侵占去大部分的夜。夜仿佛纸浸了油，变成半透明体；它给太阳拥抱住了，分不出身来，也许是给太阳陶醉了，所以夕照霞隐褪后的夜色也带着酡红。到红消醉醒，船舱里的睡人也一身腻汗地醒来，洗了澡赶到甲板上吹海风，又是一天开始。

（《围城》，钱钟书）

英语译文

　　The Red Sea had long since been crossed, and the ship was now on its way over the Indian Ocean; but as always the sun mercilessly rose early and set late, encroaching upon the better part of the night. The night, like paper soaked in oil, had become translucent. Locked in the embrace of the sun, the night's own form was indiscernible. Perhaps it had become intoxicated by the sun, which would explain why the night sky remained flushed long after the gradual fading of the rosy sunset. By the time the ruddiness dissipated and the night itself awoke from its stupor, the passengers in their cabins had awakened, glistening with sweat;

after bathing, they hurried out on deck to catch the ocean breeze. Another day had begun.

(*Fortress Besieged*, Jeanne Kelly & Nathan K. Mao 译)

| 解　析

　　同理,在此文学段落中,我们可以看到,译者在英语译文中添加了众多的定冠词。

2. 内容增补

一般来说,汉译英中,内容增补包括两方面的内容:一是文化背景知识的增补;二是逻辑成分的增补。

(1) 文化背景知识的增补

在翻译实践中,有时如果不添加相应的文化背景知识或做出一般性的阐释,原文中具有一定文化特色的隐喻、典故等成分在译入目标语时就无法被目标语读者理解。在这种情形下,译者就需要在译文中对原文的文化背景知识进行增补。

┃ 例4-28

中文原文

　　同时,我国经济发展进入新常态,正处在爬坡过坎的关口,体制机制弊端和结构性矛盾是"拦路虎",不深化改革和调整经济结构,就难以实现平稳健康发展。

(《2015年政府工作报告》)

英语译文

At the same time, China's economic development has entered a new normal. Our country is in a crucial period during which challenges need to be overcome and problems need to be resolved. Systemic, institutional, and structural problems have become "tigers in the road" holding up development. Without deepening reform and making economic structural adjustments, we will have a difficult time sustaining steady and sound development.

(*Report on the Work of the Government, 2015*)

| 解　析

　　该例中,英译文将"'拦路虎'"译为了"'tigers in the road' holding up development",不仅保留了原文使用的隐喻,还添加了对该隐喻的语义解释,即进行了内容增补。这是因为,"tigers in the road"这一隐喻在英语中较难触发障碍物的语义内容,所以需进行内容增补,消除目标语读者的理解障碍。

例4-29

中文原文

搬迁扶贫

英语译文

poverty alleviation by relocating the impoverished population from inhospitable areas to places with better economic prospects

（本例来自黄友义讲座"学深悟透、精准翻译、有效传播
——参加党政文献翻译的体会"，苏州大学，2021年11月17日）

解 析

很显然，与中文原文相比，英语译文增补了较多内容。这是因为，如果仅仅将"搬迁扶贫"译为"poverty alleviation by relocating"，可能会引起英语读者的误会：为何搬迁就能扶贫呢？这里的"搬迁扶贫"实际上指的是把贫困人口从不适合人类居住的地区搬往比较方便的、更适合人类居住的地方，从而改善人们的生活条件。译者在英译文中对相关的文化背景知识进行增补，则可以消除误会，帮助目标语读者理解原文含义。

例4-30

中文原文

如果任由这些问题蔓延开来，后果不堪设想，那就有可能发生毛泽东同志所形象比喻的"霸王别姬"了。

（《习近平谈治国理政》）

英语译文

If we allow these problems to spread like weeds, the consequences will be disastrous, and the tragedy of *Farewell My Concubine*, which Mao Zedong used as a metaphor for losing power, may come true.

(*The Governance of China*)

解 析

"霸王别姬"是我国文化中特有的典故。若不进行语义阐释，英语读者会一头雾水，不知何义。

例4-31

中文原文

稳定粮食生产,扩大油料种植面积,增加重要紧缺农产品供应,大规模开展粮棉糖高产创建,大规模开展园艺产品生产和畜牧水产养殖标准化创建,保障"米袋子""菜篮子"安全。

（《2010年政府工作报告》）

英语译文

We will keep grain production stable; expand the total area sown with oilseed; increase supplies of important agricultural products in short supply; implement a large-scale effort to increase the production of grain, cotton, oilseed, and sugar; standardize farming practices in horticulture, animal husbandry, and aquaculture; and ensure the security of the "rice bag" (grain supply) and "vegetable basket" (non-staple food supply).

（*Report on the Work of the Government, 2010*）

解析

"米袋子""菜篮子"属于我国政治语言中的行话(jargon),直接翻译,不做内容增补,外国受众是难以理解的。"米袋子",指的是粮食问题,包括粮食的种植、收购、运销和市场价格的调控;而"菜篮子",则指城镇居民蔬菜及肉蛋禽鱼等农副产品的供应。因此,译者一方面保留了原文中的概念隐喻来宣传中国政府的政策,另一方面为了避免译入目标语后产生语义上的偏差,如目标语读者很可能会将"vegetable basket"单纯理解为蔬菜的供应,又采用了注释的方法对"米袋子""菜篮子"进行增补翻译,进一步解释说明这一政策,既准确传递了该政治文本中的概念隐喻信息,又让外国受众更容易理解和接受。

(2) 逻辑成分的增补

多数情况下,汉语呈现的是隐含逻辑,而英语则呈现显性逻辑。因此,汉译英中,有些逻辑成分若不进行增补,得到的英译文读起来就易使人感觉逻辑不通。译者需对比原文和译文,增补必要的逻辑成分。

例4-32

中文原文

一乐说:"爹,这井太高了,我不敢往下跳;爹,这井太高了,我下去以后爬不上来。

爹,你找一根麻绳绑在我的腰上,把我一点一点放下去,我扎一个猛子,能扎一分钟二十三秒,我去把木桶抓住,你再把我提上来。"

许三观一听,心想一乐这崽子的主意还真不错,就跑回家去找了一根崭新的麻绳,他不敢用旧麻绳,万一一乐也像木桶那样被井水吃了进去,那可真是完蛋了。

许三观将一根麻绳的两头从一乐两条大腿那里绕过来,又系在了一乐腰里的裤带上,然后把一乐往井里一点一点放下去……这时三乐又摇摇摆摆地过来了,许三观看到三乐走过来,就说:

"三乐,你走开,你会掉到井里去的。"

(《许三观卖血记》,余华)

英语译文

Yile said, "Dad, the well's too deep. I'm scared to jump. Dad, the well's too deep, I'm scared I wouldn't be able to get back out. Dad, get some rope to tie to my waist. Let me down little by little, and then I'll dive in. I can dive for one minute and twenty-three seconds. I'll find the bucket, and then you can pull me up."

Xu Sanguan, slowly coming to the realization that Yile's plan might actually work, ran home to grab a length of brand-new rope. He was afraid that if he fastened him with a piece of old rope, Yile might disappear down the well just like the bucket. That would really be the end.

Xu Sanguan wound the two ends of the rope around Yile's thighs and then fastened the rope to his own belt. Just as he began to let Yile slide slowly down into the well, Sanle came wobbling over toward them. As soon as he approached, Xu Sanguan warned him, "Sanle, go away! You might fall down the well."

Sanle stood quietly to one side as the rope, and Yile with it, slid deeper and deeper into the well. Soon the rope went taut and tugged sharply at Xu Sanguan's belt.

Xu Sanguan began to slowly and softly count the seconds to himself as Sanle, mouth agape, looked on. "Ten seconds ... twenty seconds ... thirty seconds ... forty seconds ..." Xu Sanguan paused to take a deep breath and continued, "Fifty seconds ... sixty seconds ... one minute and ten seconds ..."

There was a sudden sharp tug on his belt that dragged Xu Sanguan a step closer to the mouth of the well. He braced his feet against the stone steps and began to pull with all his might on the rope. Sanle took up the count where his father had left off, sounding out the seconds as Xu Sanguan panted with the effort of pulling the rope up from the depths: "One minute and eleven seconds ... one minute and fifteen seconds ... one minute and twenty seconds ..." Xu Sanguan heard what sounded like the distant echo of a heavy stone falling into the water, and then a gasp and a splutter as Yile emerged above the surface of the water.

Dripping wet, he clambered the last few steps out of the well and shouted through pale blue lips, "Dad, I found the bucket! Dad, I almost couldn't hold my breath long enough! Dad, the bucket was caught under a ledge! Dad, how long was I down in the well?"

Sanle ran eagerly forward to announce the total but was quickly and dismissively waved away by Xu Sanguan, who was stroking the water from Yile's forehead with his other hand.

"Sanle, didn't I already tell you to get out of here?"

(*Chronicle of a Blood Merchant*, Andrew F. Jones 译)

解　析

这是余华的小说《许三观卖血记》中的一段,讲的是许三观不小心把木桶掉进了井里,一乐提出让许三观用绳子系住他,把他放到井里去把桶捞起来。原文中,对捞木桶的这个过程一带而过,而英译文中却加入了几段详细的描写:因为一乐说他可以在水中憋气"一分钟二十三秒",所以译文增加了他进入井下后许三观一直在仔细地为他计时的情节;译文还添加了一段三乐在许三观停止计时后继续为一乐计时的描述,将整个过程叙述得有头有尾、生动形象。在英语读者来看,如果不添加这几段描写,就无法和前面一乐说他可以在水中憋气"一分钟二十三秒"相呼应,就不合逻辑。译者安道(Andrew F. Jones)曾解释道,添加这几段描写事实上是编辑提出来的,因为原文的叙述不够清晰,没有清楚地表述事情的发展过程和结果,编辑希望余华能再补充一下;余华表示译者可以加上一段他认为合适而且完整的叙述,译者将添加的段落回译成中文以征求余华的意见,也得到了他的认可。以下是译者安道对这一过程的回忆:"I do remember that the additions I made to the scene with Yile down in the well were prompted by the US editor, who felt that the scene was unclear and insufficiently developed and requested further delineation from Yu Hua. I asked Yu Hua what to do, and he told me to go ahead and make a few minor additions as I saw fit. I remember translating the changes back into Chinese for his approval, and that he liked them."

例4-33

中文原文

郑士杰说:"你们不知道你们捡到的那张软盘,对我有多重要。我一定要……反正你们得跟我走。"

他们坐上了郑士杰的大奔驰,那感觉真好……

(《淘气包马小跳:四个调皮蛋》,杨红樱)

英语译文

Jason Zheng quickly cut the boys off, then said: "You have no idea how important that CD is. What can I do for you, in return?"

Mo desperately wanted a ride in the Mercedes Benz, so Mr. Zheng rang all the boys' parents and asked if that would be all right. Penguin's father knew Mr. Zheng through his business dealings, and said he was a good man. He reassured Monkey, Mo and Hippo's parents that their sons would be OK.

So the boys went for a ride in Jason Zheng's spacious Mercedes, which felt incredible! ...

(*Mo's Mischief: Four Troublemakers*, HarperCollins Publishers 组织翻译)

解 析

该例选自杨红樱的儿童文学作品《淘气包马小跳：四个调皮蛋》，由英国哈珀·柯林斯出版集团（HarperCollins Publishers）组织翻译成英文版，2011年在伦敦出版。该作品讲述马小跳和他的三个好朋友有一天放学后在一间公共厕所捡到一张软盘，根据软盘上的信息找到了失主——一家大公司的董事长。这张软盘对于公司十分重要，为了答谢四位小朋友，董事长决定带他们去兜风。在中文原版中，作者将写作重点放在马小跳和他的朋友做了一件好事并得到了回报，以此来宣传乐于助人的精神，帮助儿童读者树立正确的价值观。然而在英译版本中，译者增加了一段描写来说明董事长带他们去兜风前征得了四位小朋友家长的同意。这段描述在篇幅本就不长的故事中相对来说较长，译者的这种安排使之成为一个重要的故事情节。这一情节的添加对于培养儿童读者的安全意识十分重要。

例4-34

中文原文

气候与环境变化已成为人类社会生存与发展的巨大挑战。重新思考人与自然的关系，加快形成低碳、绿色的发展和生活方式，促进人类社会可持续发展，比以往任何时候都更为重要。科技，尤其是数字化，扮演了越来越重要的角色。

(《华为投资控股有限公司2020年可持续发展报告》)

英语译文

Climate change has become a formidable roadblock to our ongoing development as a society. Now more than ever, we need to reassess our relationship with nature and move faster towards low-carbon development and green growth models.

Fortunately, technology can help. In particular, digital technology is playing an increasingly important role in this process.

(*Huawei Investment & Holding Co., Ltd. 2020 Sustainability Report*)

解 析

在此段中,谈及了两个主题:一个是人与自然的关系,一个是科技的作用。在英语译文中,译者在两个主题之间增补了 "Fortunately, technology can help.",起到了逻辑衔接的作用,使两个主题间的过渡更顺畅、更合逻辑。

练习题

1. 译文补充

下列句子摘自《新时代的中国青年》白皮书,请根据原文语义将以下译文补充完整,注意省略与增补译法的运用。

(1) 青年是整个社会力量中最积极、最有生气的力量,国家的希望在青年,民族的未来在青年。中国青年始终是实现中华民族伟大复兴的先锋力量。

Youth is _____.

_____.

Young Chinese _____

_____.

(2) 五四运动前后,一大批率先接受新思想、新文化、新知识的有志青年在反复比较中选择了马克思列宁主义,促进中国人民和中华民族实现了自鸦片战争以来的第一次全面觉醒。

_____, a large number of

_____

assumed the lead in accepting new ideas, new culture, and new knowledge. After

_____ they chose to follow

Marxism-Leninism, which led to a widespread awakening of the people and the nation for the first time since the Opium War.

(3) 新时代中国青年刚健自信、胸怀天下、担当有为,衷心拥护党的领导,奋力走在时代前列,展现出前所未有的昂扬风貌;追求远大理想,心中铭刻着对马克思主义的崇高信仰、对共产主义和中国特色社会主义的坚定信念;深植家国情怀,与国家同呼吸、与人民共命运,时刻彰显着鲜明的爱国主义精神气质;传承奋斗担当,先天下之忧而忧、后天下之乐而乐,勇做走在时代前列的奋进者、开拓者、奉献者。

Young Chinese people in the new era are _____.

They wholeheartedly support the leadership of the Party. _____:

pursuing lofty ideals with _____;

full of patriotism, _____;

displaying the sterling quality of living up to responsibilities; _____

_____; striving to be _____

_____.

(4) 历史清晰而深刻地昭示,没有中国共产党就没有朝气蓬勃的中国青年运动,矢志不渝跟党走是中国青年百年奋斗的最宝贵经验,深深融入血脉的红色基因是中国青年百年奋斗的最宝贵财富。

History shows clearly that without the CPC, _____.

For China's youth, commitment to the CPC is _____

_____, and _____

_____.

(5) 中国梦是历史的、现实的,也是未来的;是广大人民的,更是青年一代的。新时代中国青年必将以永不懈怠的精神状态、永不停滞的前进姿态,在接续奋斗中将中华民族伟大复兴的中国梦变为现实。

The Chinese Dream _____.

It is _____.

China's youth in the new era will _____,

to turn the Chinese Dream of national rejuvenation into reality.

2. 句子翻译

将下列句子译为英文,注意省略和增补译法的运用。

(1) 北京市在服务和融入新发展格局的紧要处落好"五子",即建设国际科技创新中心、推进"两区"建设、发展数字经济、以供给侧结构性改革引领和创造新需求、深入推动以疏解北京非首都功能为"牛鼻子"的京津冀协同发展。

（2）我们应摒弃意识形态划线，团结起来为促进世界和平与发展事业凝聚最大公约数，画出最大同心圆。

（3）为政以德，譬如北辰，居其所而众星共之。

（4）授人以鱼，更要授人以渔。中方将积极实施"非洲人才计划"，未来3年将为非洲国家培训3万名各类人才，提供1.8万个奖学金留学生名额，加强对非洲技术转让和经验共享。

（5）江山就是人民，人民就是江山。中国共产党领导人民打江山、守江山，守的是人民的心。

（6）在2014年3月埃博拉病毒肆虐非洲大地的时候，一些国家从西非疫区三国关闭大使馆、撤离外交官和本国公民。中国政府第一时间驰援非洲，不仅送去抗疫急需物资，还派出超过1 000人次的军民医疗队奔赴疫情最严重地区。中国大使馆、外交官和医疗专家都选择了坚守，与当地人民昼夜并肩作战，直至取得抗击埃博拉疫情的最终胜利。

（7）积极发展文化事业和文化产业。推动重大文化惠民项目建设，广播电视"村村通"工程向"户户通"升级。

_____

_____

_____

（8）"立善法于天下，则天下治；立善法于一国，则一国治。"要坚持立法先行，坚持立改废释并举，加快完善法律、行政法规、地方性法规体系，完善包括市民公约、乡规民约、行业规章、团体章程在内的社会规范体系，为全面推进依法治国提供基本遵循。

_____

_____

_____

⬛ 3. 段落翻译

以下段落摘自第三十二届韩素音国际翻译大赛竞赛原文，请将其翻译为英文，注意省略与增补译法的运用。

英国哲学家罗素说过："中国至高无上的伦理品质中的一些东西，现代世界极为需要。"中华优秀传统文化所蕴含的思想观念、人文精神、道德规范，不仅涵养了中国人的精神生活、架构起中华民族的心灵空间，也对解决人类共同面临的问题具有重要价值。从"道法自然""天人合一"的发展理念，到"协和万邦""讲信修睦"的世界想象，再到"同舟共济""休戚与共"的命运共同体意识，这些由中华优秀传统文化不断滋养润泽的伦理品质，在世界各地激发更多共鸣，为解决人类共同面临的问题提供了"新的可能"。这正是春节文化在世界各地广受欢迎的深层次原因。

_____

_____

_____

第五章

移植与改写

移植与改写是两种相对应的翻译方法。移植译法主要包括概念的移植与中文中俗语和习语等表达方式的移植。改写译法根据内容上改写的幅度大小又可分为内科式改写和外科式改写。

一、移植译法在汉译英中的应用

翻译是引入或传播异域知识和异域文化的重要方式。当异域的概念、风俗文化、俚语行话等在目标语中难以找到对应成分时,译者往往就会采取移植的翻译方法。移植的主要方式就是音译,也就是通常所说的零翻译。这在我国古代就已有之,特别是到了佛经翻译时期,音译法得到了极大的发展。佛经翻译与以前的翻译存在一个重大区别,就是译文中存在大量的音译词。我国翻译理论中音译理论成熟的标志就是玄奘提出的"五不翻"理论:

> 一秘密故,如陀罗尼。二含多义故,如薄伽梵具六义。三此无故,如阎浮树,中夏实无此木。四顺古故,如阿耨菩提,非不可翻,而摩腾以来,常存梵音。五生善故,如般若尊重,智慧轻浅。而七迷之作,乃谓释迦牟尼,此名能仁,能仁之义,位卑周孔。阿耨菩提,名正遍知,此土老子之教,先有无上正真之道,无以为异。菩提萨埵名大,道心众生,其名下劣,皆掩而不翻。

"五不翻"即在五种情况下不意译,而是采取音译的方法处理原文。第一种情况指的是具有神秘色彩的词语、咒语等不用意译,而应采用音译。例如,"阿弥陀佛"具有佛语神秘、庄重和典雅的特点,但如果按照字面意思翻译成汉语,则会失去这种神秘感,失去原有的佛意。第二种情况指的是具有多种含义的词语不用意译,而应采用音译。例如,"薄伽梵"具有六种意义:自在、炽盛、端严、名称、吉祥、尊贵,汉语里不存在同时包含这六种意义的对应词汇。如果采取意译,在一定的语境中只能译出其中的一个意义,而其余五种意义都会缺失,故此只能选择音译。第三种情况指的是目标语文化中没有的词语不用意译,而应采用音译。例如,"阎浮树"(又名"胜金树")只产于印度等地,中国没有这种树,所以采用音译。第四种情况指的是对以前已经存在并广泛使用的、约定俗成的音译词语不用意译,而应遵循习惯沿袭其原有的音译。例如,"阿耨菩提"可以翻译为"无上""正等""正觉"。但从东汉佛教传入我国以来历代佛经翻译家都采用梵语的音译,所以玄奘法师认为不需采用意译,而应保持其约定俗成的音译。第五种情况指的是有些词语的音译能令人生尊重之念,否则容易等闲视之,所以对这类词语不用意译,而应采用音译。例如,"般若"跟汉语里的"智慧"意思差不多,但有着轻重之分。

汉译英中的移植,主要包括概念的移植与中文中俗语、习语等表达方式的移植。

1. 概念的移植

概念的移植,指的是我国哲学、政治、中医等知识领域中特有的概念在英语世界中找不到合适的对应语,所以采取音译的方式进行翻译。

| 例5-1

中文原文

阴者,藏精而起亟也,阳者,卫外而为固也。阴不胜其阳,则脉流薄疾,并乃狂。阳不胜其阴,则五脏气争,九窍不通。是以圣人陈阴阳,筋脉和同,骨髓坚固,气血皆从。如是则内外调和,邪不能害,耳目聪明,气立如故。

(《黄帝内经·素问》)

英语译文

Yin is the essence of the organs and the fountain of the *qi. Yang* protects the exterior of the body against pathogens and makes the muscles function. When the *yin* fails to contain the *yang*, the flow in the channels will become rapid, causing the *yang qi* to become excessive and reckless. If the *yang qi* is deficient and unable to counterbalance the *yin*, communication between the internal organs will be disrupted, and the nine orifices will cease to function. The sages, who understood the principles of *yin* and *yang*, were able to let their bodies perform all functions harmoniously. When *yin* and *yang* are balanced, the five *zang* organs function appropriately together; the tendons, ligaments, vessels, channels, and collaterals all flow smoothly; the muscles, bones, and marrow are abundant and strong, *qi* and blood follow the right path, internal and external are synergetic, vision is clear, and hearing is acute. Thus the *zhen*/true *qi* becomes unshakable, and pathogens cannot invade.

(*The Yellow Emperor's Classic of Medicine*, 倪毛信译)

| 解　析

这段话讲述的是人体中的阴阳与人的健康之间的关系。阴、阳、气等是我国古代哲学家、中医基于对宇宙、人体等的认识而提出的概念,迥异于西方的哲学与医学思想。这些概念在英语世界找不到对应词,因此倪毛信在翻译《黄帝内经》时采取了移植的方式,即音译。如果对这些概念进行意译,很可能就会误传我国中医中的重要概念。

例5-2

中文原文

她是在寻死呢！那痨病病人此时已经钻到了人堆里，他在人堆里高声说，五谷城的好**风水**，一定被她哭破了，这女子，犯了杀头之罪啦！

（《碧奴：孟姜女哭长城的传说》，苏童）

英语译文

"She's just begging to die," exclaimed the consumptive, who had threaded his way back through the crowd, "Her tears have ruined Five-Grain City's excellent *fengshui* and for that she should lose her head."

（*Binu and the Great Wall*, Howard Goldblatt 译）

解　析

"风水"是我国古代玄学的重要概念，历史悠久，内涵丰富。在英语世界中，没有对应性概念，所以葛浩文在此也采取了移植译法，即音译。

2. 中文中俗语、习语等表达方式的移植

翻译文学文本时，采用移植译法处理中文中俗语、习语等表达方式往往有两种目的：一是体现翻译文本的异质性，让读者明显感觉到所读的文本是翻译文本；二是在允许的范围内传播中国文化。与增补译法不同，移植译法翻译俗语、习语一般适用于直接翻译而不引起误解的情形，这样有利于向目标语引入异质文化元素。

例5-3

中文原文

碧奴说，那是我的袍子的声音，我**风餐露宿**的，瘦得厉害，我的袍子变得又肥又大，一走路风就灌进来了。

（《碧奴：孟姜女哭长城的传说》，苏童）

英语译文

That was the sound of my clothing. I eat in the wind and sleep in the dew, and I have grown thin. My clothing now fits much too loosely and, when I walk, the wind blows through it.

（*Binu and the Great Wall*, Howard Goldblatt 译）

> **解 析**
>
> "风餐露宿"是汉语中的习惯性表达方式,字面意思是"在风里就餐,露天睡觉",实际形容旅途或生活很艰辛。在英语中,无此表达方式,但葛浩文还是按字面意思将其译为"eat in the wind and sleep in the dew",进而带来阅读上的异质性。

例5-4

中文原文

南边也出美人呀?你们看她<u>蛾眉凤眼杨柳腰</u>的,是个美人么。

(《碧奴:孟姜女哭长城的传说》,苏童)

英语译文

I didn't know there were beauties down south too. Just look at <u>her delicate moth eyebrows, her phoenix eyes and her willowy waist</u>, a classic beauty.

(Binu and the Great Wall, Howard Goldblatt 译)

> **解 析**
>
> 同理,英语中很少用"蛾眉凤眼杨柳腰"来描述一个人,但葛浩文直接将这一表达移植到了英语译文中,将其译为"her delicate moth eyebrows, her phoenix eyes and her willowy waist"。"峨眉""凤眼""杨柳腰"这些词语都是汉语中用来描述人物外貌的特有词汇,译者采用移植译法,将具有中国特色的表达移植到了英语中,使译文更加生动形象。

例5-5

中文原文

他们怀着嫉妒心说起平原地区的繁荣和富庶,并非那里的人有<u>三头六臂</u>,一切都是一马平川带来的福运。

(《碧奴:孟姜女哭长城的传说》,苏童)

英语译文

Many of the residents of her village had travelled to the plains and returned filled with envious stories of the splendour and richness of those places, whose residents did not, as foretold, <u>have three heads and six arms</u>, but were graced with the good fortune of vast land holdings.

(Binu and the Great Wall, Howard Goldblatt 译)

| 解　析

在汉语中,"三头六臂"是一种习惯性说法,表示一个人神通广大。葛浩文采用移植译法,将其译为"have three heads and six arms"。

例5-6

中文原文

有钱才能使鬼推磨,你身上还有刀币吗?

(《碧奴:孟姜女哭长城的传说》,苏童)

英语译文

But money can make the Devil turn a millstone. Do you have any sabre coins left?

(*Binu and the Great Wall*, Howard Goldblatt 译)

| 解　析

"有钱才能使鬼推磨"是汉语里的一个俗语,形容金钱万能。葛浩文采用移植译法,将此习语译为"but money can make the Devil turn a millstone",同时也将其中蕴含的文化思想移植到了译入语中。

例5-7

中文原文

戊戌乱党,在京伏法,钱犯兔死狐悲,丧心病狂,竟于本年十月十一日,阴谋刺杀首长,幸天佑我军,令袁大人无恙。

(《檀香刑》,莫言)

英语译文

When the Wuxu rebels were executed in the capital, like the fox that mourns the death of the hare, the frenzied Qian made an attempt on the life of our commander on the eleventh day of the tenth month. Heaven interceded to spare the life of Excellency Yuan.

(*Sandalwood Death*, Howard Goldblatt 译)

| 解　析

"兔死狐悲"是汉语中的一个习语,比喻因同类的死亡或失败而感到悲伤。葛浩文采用移植的翻译方法,将汉语中这一隐喻性的说法直接移植到了英语译文中,译为"like the fox that mourns the death of the hare"。

例5-8

中文原文

咱家把锅灶里的火弄小，往锅里加了油。然后把两根宝贝橛子小心翼翼地放了进去。咱家提醒自己：赵甲，你要仔细啊！人过留名，雁过留声，只有圆满地完成了这次檀香刑，你才能成为名副其实的刽子状元。如果完不成这次檀香刑，你的一世英名就完了。

（《檀香刑》，莫言）

英语译文

I lowered the fire under the cauldron and added oil. Then I carefully put my precious spears back into the cauldron, reminding myself, Pay attention, Old Zhao. Wild geese leave behind their cry; men leave behind a name. You need only carry out this sandalwood execution with perfection to live up to your designation as the *zhuangyuan* of executioners. If you fail, your name will die with you.

(*Sandalwood Death*, Howard Goldblatt 译)

解析

"人过留名，雁过留声"也是汉语中的习语，表示人虽然走了，其名却让人难以忘怀，如同大雁飞去，留下其鸣之声。葛浩文将这一汉语习语直接译为"wild geese leave behind their cry; men leave behind a name"，同时也将中国特有的文化表达移植到了英语中。

例5-9

中文原文

俺爹的嗓子，沙瓤的西瓜，不知道迷倒过高密东北乡多少女人。俺那死去的娘就是迷上了他的公鸭嗓子才嫁给他做了老婆。

（《檀香刑》，莫言）

英语译文

His voice, soft and pliable, like watermelon pulp, captivated scores of Northeast Gaomi Township beauties, including my late *niang*, who married him solely on the strength of his voice.

(*Sandalwood Death*, Howard Goldblatt 译)

> **解　析**
>
> 　　将沙哑的嗓子比作"沙瓤的西瓜"是莫言独创的隐喻表达。葛浩文采用移植翻译方法，将其直接译为"his voice, soft and pliable, like watermelon pulp"，也将莫言新创的这一汉语表达移植到了英语中。

例5-10

中文原文

　　主簿陈琳曰："不可！俗云：掩目而捕燕雀，是自欺也，微物尚不可欺以得志，况国家大事乎？今将军仗皇威，掌兵要，龙骧虎步，高下在心：若欲诛宦官，如鼓洪炉燎毛发耳。但当速发雷霆，行权立断，则天人顺之。却反外檄大臣，临犯京阙，英雄聚会，各怀一心：所谓倒持干戈，授人以柄，功必不成，反生乱矣。"

（《三国演义》，罗贯中）

英语译文

　　But Chen Lin, first secretary to He Jin, objected: "That's not going to work! You know the proverb, 'You can't catch a sparrow with your eyes shut.' Even trivial ends cannot be gained by self-deception; what of affairs of state? Now, General, you have the weight of the throne behind you and military authority in your hands. You can 'prance like a dragon and prowl like a tiger'. Whatever you wish is yours. You can execute the eunuchs as easily as you can burn a hair in a furnace. Act with lightning speed, with decision and expedition, and the whole world will go along. There's no need to call in outside forces and bring a mob of warriors down on the capital, each with his own ambitions. That is like handing someone a weapon pointed toward yourself! You will fail, and worse, you will create an upheaval."

(Three Kingdoms: A Historical Novel, Moss Roberts 译)

> **解　析**
>
> 　　在中文原文中，我们看到，"掩目而捕燕雀""龙骧虎步""鼓洪炉燎毛发耳""倒持干戈"都属中文中的特有表达方式。译者罗慕士（Moss Roberts）采用移植译法，分别将这些汉语表达译为"catch a sparrow with your eyes shut""prance like a dragon and prowl like a tiger""burn a hair in a furnace""handing someone a weapon pointed toward yourself"，同时也将中国特有的文化移植到了英语中。

　　在政治文本翻译中，也有采用移植译法翻译中文中俗语、习语等表达方式的情况。其目的主要是传播中国文化。

例5-11

中文原文

星星之火,可以燎原。

（《毛泽东选集》）

英语译文

A single spark can start a prairie fire.

(*Selected Works of Mao Tse-Tung*)

解　析

"星星之火,可以燎原",比喻新生事物尽管开始时力量微小,但有远大发展前途。这里的翻译完整地移植了原文的习语性表达,并没有翻译为其引申的含义。

例5-12

中文原文

"蛋糕"不断做大了,同时还要把"蛋糕"分好。

（《习近平谈治国理政》）

英语译文

Even when the "cake" has indeed become bigger, we must cut it fairly.

(*The Governance of China*)

解　析

本句话的意思是在注重生产的同时,要缩小贫富差距,这样才能稳步实现全面小康与共同富裕。"蛋糕"一词在有些译文里被翻译成"pie",但在此处译者选择了更加忠实于原文的"cake",虽然外国读者更加熟悉"pie",知道其中蕴含的分配之意,但是蛋糕也来源于外国,所以外国读者对"cake"并不会感到陌生。

例5-13

中文译文

空谈误国,实干兴邦。

（《习近平谈治国理政》）

英语译文

Empty talk harms the country, while hard work makes it flourish.

(The Governance of China)

> **解　析**
>
> 　　这是习近平主席在"十三五"时期对各级领导班子与领导干部提出的要求。他提出要实现全面小康的蓝图,就需要一步一步、脚踏实地地劳动,切实地干出实效来。此处,译者选择了移植式的翻译,将原语中有关中国优良传统文化和脚踏实地、勤劳务实的精神的表达移植到了译入语中。

二、改写译法在汉译英中的应用

翻译作为改写,这是文化学派学者勒弗维尔(Lefevere)提出的翻译理念,也称为对翻译的操纵。显然,这种翻译方式对原文的改动幅度较大。勒弗维尔(1992)指出,翻译中的改写主要受到两方面的制约:一是意识形态的制约,指的是政治、经济、社会等方面对翻译中的改写所施加的影响;二是诗学的制约,指的是目标语文化体系对翻译中的改写所施加的影响。根据翻译中改写的程度,可将翻译中的改写分为两大类:一是内科式改写,即小幅度的改写,内容上不做大幅度的改动,但形式上有所调整;二是外科式改写,即在内容上做大幅度的改动,有时甚至是改头换面。

1. 内科式改写

例 5-14

中文原文

　　大河这边,就葵花一个孩子。

　　葵花很孤独,是那种一只鸟拥有万里天空而却看不见另外任何一只鸟的孤独。这只鸟在空阔的天空下飞翔着,只听见翅膀划过气流时发出的寂寞声。苍苍茫茫,无边无际。各种形状的云彩,浮动在它的四周。有时,天空干脆光光溜溜,没有一丝痕迹,像巨大的青石板。实在寂寞时,它偶尔会鸣叫一声,但这鸣叫声,直衬得天空更加的空阔,它的心更加的孤寂。

(《青铜葵花》,曹文轩)

英语译文

　　On this side of the river there were no other children but Sunflower. She was alone, like a solitary bird in a vast blue sky with nothing for company but the sound of its own beating wings. In a sky that stretches on for ever, <u>broken occasionally by a cloud or two</u>, but otherwise huge and unblemished, like a perfect turquoise <u>gemstone</u>. At moments of extreme loneliness the bird cries out, but its cry only makes the sky seem even emptier.

(*Bronze and Sunflower*, Helen Wang 译)

解　析

　　这是著名儿童文学家曹文轩的《青铜葵花》中的一个段落。表面看来,译文和原文好像很是对应。但通过仔细对比,我们可以发现,译者王海岚(Helen Wang)根据英语的表达需要,改写或省略了中文原文中下划线的部分,如将"青石板"改写为了"宝石"("gemstone")。同时,也对原文的结构进行了调整:两段合并为了一段;第二、三句合并为英译文中的第二句,第四、五句合并为了英译文中的第三句。整体来看,该段译文对原文进行了小幅度的改写,主要为形式上的调整,属内科式改写。

例5-15

中文原文

　　这个人打扮与众姑娘不同,彩绣辉煌,恍若神妃仙子:头上戴着金丝八宝攒珠髻,绾着朝阳五凤挂珠钗;项上带着赤金盘螭璎珞圈;裙边系着豆绿宫绦双鱼比目玫瑰佩;身上穿着缕金百蝶穿花大红洋缎窄裉袄,外罩五彩刻丝石青银鼠褂;下着翡翠撒花洋绉裙。一双丹凤三角眼,两弯柳叶吊梢眉,身量苗条,体格风骚,粉面含春威不露,丹唇未启笑先闻。

(《红楼梦》,曹雪芹)

英语译文

She was dressed quite differently from the others present, gleaming like some fairy princess with sparkling jewels and gay embroideries.

Her chignon was enclosed in a circlet of gold filigree and clustered pearls. It was fastened with a pin embellished with flying phoenixes, from whose beaks pearls were suspended on tiny chains.

Her necklet was of red gold in the form of a coiling dragon.

Her dress had a fitted bodice and was made of dark red silk damask with a pattern of flowers and butterflies in raised gold thread.

Her jacket was lined with ermine. It was of a slate-blue stuff with woven insets in coloured silks.

Her under-skirt was of a turquoise-coloured imported silk crêpe embroidered with flowers.

She had, moreover,

eyes like a painted phoenix,

eyebrows like willow-leaves,

a slender form,

seductive grace;

the ever-smiling summer face

of hidden thunders showed no trace;

the ever-bubbling laughter started

almost before the lips were parted.

(The Story of the Stone, David Hawkes 译)

> **解 析**
>
> 　　霍克斯的译文主要是将原文的分句各自为段,使之更清晰,即调整了结构,但内容改动不多。

例 5-16

中文原文

谁影响华为?

华为对外依靠客户与合作伙伴,坚持以客户为中心,通过创新的产品为客户创造价值;对内依靠努力奋斗的员工,以奋斗者为本,让有贡献者得到合理回报;并与合作伙伴、产业组织、开源社区、标准组织、大学、研究机构等构建共赢的生态圈,推动技术进步和产业发展;我们遵从业务所在国适用的法律法规,为当地社会创造就业、带来税收贡献、使能数字化,并与政府、媒体等保持开放沟通。

(《华为投资控股有限公司 2020 年可持续发展报告》)

英语译文

Who does Huawei work with?

Externally, we rely on our customers and partners. Customers are at the heart of everything we do, and we create value for them with innovative products. Internally, we rely on our hard-working and dedicated employees. At Huawei, those who contribute more get

<u>more.</u>

We work with a broad range of stakeholders including partners, industry organizations, open source communities, standards organizations, universities, and research institutes all over the world to cultivate a broader ecosystem that thrives on shared success. In this way, we can help drive advancements in technology and grow the industry as a whole.

<u>We create local employment opportunities, pay taxes, and comply with all applicable laws and regulations in the countries where we operate. We also help local industries go digital,</u> and openly engage with governments, the media, and other stakeholders.

(*Huawei Investment & Holding Co., Ltd. 2020 Sustainability Report*)

┃ 解 析

这是《华为投资控股有限公司2020年可持续发展报告》中的内容。通过比对原文与译文,我们发现译者做出了如下改变:第一,题目由"谁影响华为?"改为了"华为与谁合作?"("Who does Huawei work with?");第二,原文中的一段文字在译文中被切分为了三段;第三,对原文最后一部分的结构进行了调整,"为当地社会创造就业"在译文中被调整到了句首;第四,"让有贡献者得到合理回报"被改译为了"多劳多得"("those who contribute more get more")。因此,整体来说,译文主要在形式上有所改动,内容调整较少,属内科式改写。

---

2. 外科式改写

┃ 例5-17

中文原文

　　行者才教三个王子就于暴纱亭后,静室之间,画了罡斗,教三人都俯伏在内,一个个瞑目宁神。这里却暗暗念动真言,诵动咒语,将仙气吹入他三人心腹之中,把元神收归本舍,传与口诀,各授得万千之膂力,运添了火候,却象个脱胎换骨之法。运遍了子午周天,那三个小王子,方才苏醒,一齐爬将起来,抹抹脸,精神抖擞,一个个骨壮筋强:大王子就拿得金箍棒,二王子就轮得九齿钯,三王子就举得降妖杖。

(《西游记》,吴承恩)

英语译文

Sun told them they must acquire more power, and must first be taught <u>HOW TO PRAY</u>. He ordered the three young princes to go to a quiet room, where he drew the seven stars of the Great Bear on the floor, and made the princes kneel on them. He told them to close their eyes, concentrate their thoughts on Scripture truth, and let the breath of Heaven enter their bodies, so that God's spirit might dwell in their heart. After prayer, they would receive renewed power, being born again, their very bones being transformed, and they would become the sons of God.

(A Mission to Heaven: A Great Chinese Epic and Allegory, Timothy Richard 译)

解 析

　　这是《西游记》第八十八回中一段有关孙悟空收玉华王的三个王子为徒的故事。这本是孙悟空教三个王子练功的内容,但译者李提摩太(Timothy Richard)则完全将其改写为了基督教受礼的故事来宣传基督教,可谓是改头换面,面目全非,和原文内容大相径庭。这与译者的身份背景有关。李提摩太(1845—1919)是英国传教士,清末来我国传教,翻译了《西游记》的第一个英译本 *A Mission to Heaven: A Great Chinese Epic and Allegory*。《西游记》在我国为经典文学文本,但在李提摩太这个传教士的眼中却富含宗教意义,他借翻译佛教题材的文学作品来传播基督教精神。但由于李提摩太的译文偏离原著的本来面貌太多,也可以说是对原著的一种扭曲,使原著失去了本来的文学光彩和文化价值,因此李提摩太的译本在英语世界虽有一定的影响,但影响不大。

例 5-18

中文原文

　　几乎是在一瞬间,我胸中的怒火燃烧起来了。我从地上找到了一块碎红砖,在窗外瞄了半天,我先瞄准了赵春堂,转念一想,虽然是他拽了慧仙的辫梢,可辫子是长在慧仙头上的,她为什么不甩掉他的手呢? 她甘心做他的木偶,我就应该瞄着她。我举起碎砖瞄准了慧仙,我看见我的向日葵在小餐厅里热情地绽放,她把餐厅里的所有干部都当作太阳了,一会儿向这个太阳微笑,一会儿向那个太阳鞠躬,她的脸上起了红晕,眼波流转,我瞄准了她的脸,却怎么也下不了手,那是我秘密的向日葵啊,纵有千错万错,我不忍心砸她。我不知道自己该怎么办,最终我瞄准了餐厅气窗上那块明亮的玻璃,砰的一声脆响,一餐厅的人都回头看着气窗,趁着他们没醒过神来,我撒腿跑了。

(《河岸》,苏童)

英语译文

Flames of anger burned in my breast. I bent down, picked up a broken brick and stood at the window taking aim, first at Zhao Chuntang. How can I describe my feelings towards

Zhao? I hated him with all my heart, but I was too afraid of him to throw that brick. So I took aim at my sunflower, Huixian! All the officials in the dining hall were her suns; she'd smile at one of them, then bow to another, her cheeks flushed as she glanced round the room. But she was my secret sunflower! No matter how many mistakes she made or how badly she acted, I couldn't harm her. So what could I do? In the end, I decided to let words be my weapon. Using the brick as my writing instrument, I wrote on the wall: "ZHAO CHUNTANG IS AN ALIEN CLASS ELEMENT".

(*The Boat to Redemption*, Howard Goldblatt 译)

解 析

这是苏童的小说《河岸》中的一段话。库东亮迷上了慧仙,就鼓足了勇气来到镇上的综合大楼等慧仙。但通过食堂窗子,东亮发现一群官员在让慧仙作陪,赵春堂甚至还拽了慧仙的辫子。于是,东亮气急败坏,将一块砖头砸向了食堂的窗子。但在葛浩文的英译文中,东亮的这个行为完全被改写了:他拿起砖头,在墙上写下了"赵春堂是个异类"。在墙上写口号是当时社会上一种较为普遍的做法,在前文中东亮也经常写口号。这样的改写可能是译者出于结构上的连贯性的考虑而做出了调整。此外,原文中"转念一想,虽然是他拽了慧仙的辫梢,可辫子是长在慧仙头上的,她为什么不甩掉他的手呢?她甘心做他的木偶,我就应该瞄着她。"在译文中被改写为了"How can I describe my feelings towards Zhao? I hated him with all my heart, but I was too afraid of him to throw that brick."。译文描写了东亮虽然鼓足了勇气,但出于惧怕,没有拿起砖头砸向赵春堂,突出了东亮对赵春堂既恨又怕的心理。

例5-19

中文原文

赵春堂极其讨厌慧仙的新发型,有一次他在综合大楼的楼梯上发现那堆"马粪"在前面漂浮,一下怒不可遏,操起墙角的一把长杆竹帚,用扫帚杆子去捅慧仙头顶的"马粪",放下来,把你头上那堆马粪放下来,你在这大楼里臭美什么?慧仙惊叫着躲开了扫帚杆子,站在楼梯上拍心口,给自己压惊。赵春堂顺势把扫帚扔到了慧仙的脚下,他说你不肯穿铁梅的衣服,我没跟你计较,别以为我对你放任自流了,你是李铁梅,不是少奶奶,好好的一条辫子,不准堆得那么高!慧仙对赵春堂惧怕三分,踢走了扫帚,噘着嘴拿下七八个发卡,一点一点地把辫子放下来,放得不甘心,嘴里忍不住埋怨起来,你一个男人家,美不美的你懂什么?我的辫子又不是公共财产,你天天管着我的辫子干什么呀？赵春堂先是一愣，继而冷笑一声，你还讨厌我管你？哪天我不管你了，你不要哭鼻子！

（《河岸》,苏童）

英语译文

　　Zhao Chuntang was particularly worried. A self-possessed man, his face never betrayed his emotions, but a good many occupants of the General Affairs Building could see that he disapproved of Huixian's new hair style. He had grown used to tugging on her braid. It had become a means of exercising leadership, whether in the building's conference room or in the dining hall when he entertained guests. He made his instruction known by how he tugged the braid-to the side, downward, from the middle, or at the top. But now that Huixian's braid was stacked atop her head, when he reached behind her out of habit, what he held was not her braid but her lower back, an unintentionally inelegant and easily misconstrued action. Officials in the building frequently noticed a frown on Zhao's face. "Take it down," he'd say to Huixian, pointing at her hair. "It looks like a pile of horse dung. You don't really think it's attractive, do you? It's brazen and it's ugly."

　　Not daring to defy Zhao in public, Huixian would unclip the braid and let it hang down her back. As soon as he wasn't around, she'd coil it back up on top again and complain to anyone who would listen, "What does he know about beauty? Besides, my braid isn't public property. I don't need him to tell me what to do with it. That's my business."

(*The Boat to Redemption*, Howard Goldblatt 译)

解　析

　　慧仙因不满意原先李铁梅式的齐腰发型，就换了一个更时尚的盘头发型。但赵春堂看见后，极为不满，"一下怒不可遏，操起墙角的一把长杆竹帚，用扫帚杆子去捅慧仙头顶的'马粪'"。赵春堂是镇上的书记，不应该有这样的行为，况且这还是在公共场合。实际上，即使是普通人也不应该有这样的行为，但这也恰恰反映出当时社会上存在的荒谬现象。或许是葛浩文认为，赵春堂的行为不符合其人物的身份和地位，所以将赵春堂用扫帚杆子去捅慧仙头顶的行为改写为了言语上的劝说："把头发放下来！看上去像马粪，你还觉得这很漂亮吗？很难看。"（Take it down. It looks like a pile of horse dung. You don't really think it's attractive, do you? It's brazen and it's ugly.）此外，葛浩文在此段中间还添加了一大段文字，描述赵春堂是如何抚摸慧仙的辫子的，即 "He had grown used to ... and easily misconstrued action." 因此，可以说，葛浩文的英译文在此处的改动幅度较大，且主要是内容上的改动。

译者对慧仙的描述也进行了改写，他将原文中"嘴里忍不住埋怨起来"译为"as soon as he wasn't around, she'd coil it back up on top again and complain to anyone who would listen"，将慧仙的埋怨从当着赵春堂的面直接埋怨改写为了在背地里逢人便埋怨，更侧重表达慧仙对赵春堂惧怕三分，不敢当面表示不满。

除了内容上的改写之外，译者还对叙事视角进行了改动。例如，"Zhao Chuntang was particularly worried. A self-possessed man, his face never betrayed his emotions, but a good many occupants of the General Affairs Building could see that he disapproved of Huixian's new hair style." 以及 "Officials in the building frequently noticed a frown on Zhao's face." 等对赵春堂的描写，采用了综合大楼里其他工作人员的视角，增强了译文的叙事效果。

苏童的小说《河岸》2009年由人民文学出版社出版，获评2009年度英仕曼亚洲文学奖（Man Asian Literary Prize）。葛浩文将其译为英文，于2010年由道布尔戴出版社（Doubleday Books）出版，英文题目为 The Boat to Redemption。通过对比中英文题目，我们也可以看出，译文的改动幅度较大。葛浩文曾指出，如果将"河岸"直接译为英文 *The Bank of the River*，在英语中毫无意义（"makes no sense"）。但将题目改写为 The Boat to Redemption（救赎船），在一定程度上呼应了小说的内容，但 "redemption" 毕竟有着宗教的味道。在此意义上而言，葛浩文的译文也是对原文的扭曲，透露着其强烈的东方主义色彩。

因此，这种外科式的改写往往会造成文化及其他信息传播的失真，造成对原文的扭曲，一般不予提倡。当然，这也反映出翻译不仅仅是语言文字之间的转换，还是文化间碰撞与妥协的结果。

📑 练习题

1. 译文补充

下列句子摘自第三十二届韩素音国际翻译大赛竞赛原文。请根据原文语义将以下译文补充完整，注意移植与改写译法的运用。

（1）春节文化在世界竞相绽放，为外国人带去不一样的<u>生活烟火</u>与文化意趣。喝一碗腊八粥，体验"<u>过了腊八就是年</u>"；穿一身红衣，讨个<u>红红火火的好彩头</u>；逛一场庙会，感受中国春节热闹的氛围。

The Spring Festival culture is flourishing all over the world, bringing foreigners exotic

_____ and cultural fun.

_____,

they have come to understand a saying from a ballad: "_____

_____."

Wearing red outfits, they _____.

_____,

　they enjoy a jolly air of festivity.

（2）春联、窗花、爆竹、年夜饭、守岁酒、拜年送福，这些带着强烈仪式感的习俗，寄寓着中
　　国人对美好生活的希冀、对家庭价值的坚守、对团圆共享的追求。

Many rituals and ceremonial customs — such as _____

_____ — embody the

Chinese people's desire for a good life, adherence to family values, and pursuit of shared

reunion.

（3）"共欢新故岁，迎送一宵中"。中华文化积淀着中华民族最深沉的精神追求，是中华
　　民族生生不息、发展壮大的丰厚滋养。

"_____."

Chinese culture, the accumulation of the most profound spiritual pursuit of the Chinese nation,

serves as rich nutrition for the nation to survive and thrive.

2. 句子翻译

　　将下列句子译为英文，注意移植与改写译法的运用。

（1）我们不仅要通过发展经济，把社会财富这个"蛋糕"做大，也要通过合理的收入分配
　　制度把"蛋糕"分好。

_____

_____

_____

（2）改革开放是推动发展的制胜法宝。

（3）朝廷给出黄榜，召人医治，感动天庭，差遣太白金星下界，化作一老叟前来揭了黄榜，
自言能止太子啼哭。

（4）八月深秋，无边无际的高粱红成洸洋的血海，高粱高密辉煌，高粱凄婉可人，高粱爱情
激荡。

（5）环境污染是民生之患、民心之痛，要铁腕治理。

（6）看他如今的作品，或浓墨泼彩，恣肆汪洋；或青绿写意，画境幽邃；细微处，线条圆润
流畅，轻盈跳跃；粗放处，用笔练达，一气呵成。大自然的朴素放达，山川树木的原始
野趣，尽染纸上。

（7）"看门狗"嗷地一声叫，跳一跳，离地足有二十厘米高，喝道："兔崽子，你敢骂老子？
老子毙了你！"

B. 诗歌翻译

将下列诗歌《送友人》译为英文,注意移植与改写译法的运用。

送 友 人

李 白

青山横北郭,白水绕东城。

此地一为别,孤蓬万里征。

浮云游子意,落日故人情。

挥手自兹去,萧萧班马鸣。

参考答案

第一章　对应与转换

▣ 1. 译文补充

　　(1) ideas

　　(2) philosophy

　　(3) vision

　　(4) principle

　　(5) conviction

　　(6) values

　　(7) safe development

▣ 2. 句子翻译

　　(1) Core socialist values represent the contemporary Chinese spirit and are a crystallization of the values shared by all Chinese people.

　　(2) We will undertake extensive public awareness activities to help the people develop firm ideals and convictions, build their awareness of socialism with Chinese characteristics and the Chinese Dream, foster a Chinese ethos and a readiness to respond to the call of the times, strengthen the guiding role of patriotism, collectivism, and socialism, and see that the people develop an accurate understanding of history, ethnicity, country, and culture.

　　(3) We will uphold justice while pursuing shared interests, and will foster new thinking on common, comprehensive, cooperative, and sustainable security.

　　(4) China follows the principle of achieving shared growth through discussion and collaboration in engaging in global governance.

　　(5) We will adopt an all-encompassing approach to food, develop protected agriculture, and build a diversified food supply system.

▣ 3. 段落翻译

　　ICH (intangible cultural heritage) is an important part of the best of our traditional culture, representing the intellectual wealth of people of all ethnic groups and 5,000 years of uninterrupted

Chinese civilization. A systematic approach is therefore needed for its protection, for it to pass down and grow. Not long ago, the Fifth National List of Representative Elements of Intangible Cultural Heritage of China was published, which includes for protection a number of new items with significant historical, literary, artistic and scientific value. To date, a total of 1,557 items have been designated national-level intangible cultural heritage assets. Listing and protection mechanisms have been set up at the national, provincial, municipal and county levels. These systems, designed for the Chinese context, cover more than 100,000 ICH items. China has thus put in place fairly extensive lists, which could prove to be important resources as China interacts with other civilizations in the world.

第二章　拆分与整合

1. 译文补充

(1) and increasingly replaced the unrestrained natural landscape with well-regulated prosperity

(2) However, people should not ignore, or show a total disregard for wilderness, but to look for the best space to live in harmony with it; We need to bear in mind

(3) has been running for 5,000 years and will never dry up

(4) gets increasingly away from your childhood and then from your adolescence; You may even feel very lonely and suffer from a lot of social exclusion; To me, the way out is to keep searching for everything I'm passionate about

2. 句子翻译

(1) Chinese modernization is socialist modernization pursued under the leadership of the Communist Party of China. It contains elements that are common to the modernization processes of all countries, but it is more characterized by features that are unique to the Chinese context.

(2) Development is our Party's top priority in governing and rejuvenating China, for without solid material and technological foundations, we cannot hope to build a great modern socialist country in all respects.

(3) China attaches great importance to promoting marine ecological civilization, and is making sustained efforts to strengthen the prevention and control of marine pollution, protect marine biodiversity, and promote the orderly development and utilization of marine resources.

China also stands ready to deepen cooperation with all countries on these fronts to contribute to the green development of the ocean.

(4) Inside the threshold stood a slender young girl, with a delicate complexion, very pretty features, bright black eyes and long lashes. She stared at Little Jade in astonishment.

(5) Under most circumstances, a new look or new atmosphere in work are not related to formulating new plans or designing new slogans. Rather, they come about naturally when earnest, down-to-earth efforts are made to turn scientifically sound goals in the good blueprint into reality by taking stock of new conditions, adopting new ideas and employing new measures.

(6) Compared with the past, we have more to study today, not less, because of the new circumstances and tasks confronting us.

(7) Our study of this issue, however, should not stop just here. We need to probe deeper into it, because those engaged in market activity are individual traders, each being a resource investor.

(8) It is no easy job for a country as big as China to fully represent and address the concerns of its 1.4 billion people. It must have a robust and centralized leadership.

3. 段落翻译

At around 140 BC during China's Han Dynasty, Zhang Qian, a royal emissary, made a journey to the West from Chang'an (present-day Xi'an in Shaanxi Province), opening an overland route linking the East and the West. Centuries later, in the years of the Tang, Song and Yuan dynasties, silk routes boomed both over land and at sea, facilitating trade between the East and the West. In the early 15th century, Zheng He, the famous Chinese navigator of the Ming Dynasty, made seven voyages to the Western Seas, which boosted trade along the maritime silk routes.

For thousands of years the ancient silk routes served as major arteries of interaction, spanning the valleys of the Nile, the Tigris and Euphrates, the Indus and Ganges, and the Yellow and Yangtze rivers. They connected the birthplaces of the Egyptian, Babylonian, Indian and Chinese civilizations, the lands of the believers of Buddhism, Christianity and Islam, and the homes of peoples of different nationalities and races. These routes increased connectivity among countries on the Eurasian continent, facilitated exchanges and mutual learning between Eastern and Western civilizations, boosted regional development and prosperity, and shaped the Silk Road spirit characterized by peace and cooperation, openness and inclusiveness, mutual learning and mutual benefit.

第三章 虚化与实化

📖 1. 译文补充

(1) a cancer; the vitality; ability

(2) regular, long-term; carry forward our revolutionary traditions and heritage

(3) The times are calling us; pressing ahead with unwavering commitment and perseverance; answer the call of our times and meet the expectations of our people

(4) never deviate from; the great ship of socialism with Chinese characteristics catches the wind, cuts through the waves, and sails steadily into the future

(5) all living things may grow side by side without harming one another, and different roads may run in parallel without interfering with one another; pursue the cause of common good

📖 2. 句子翻译

(1) Of course, as practice evolves continuously, our thoughts and work should keep up with the changing times, and when we are absolutely sure, we can make adjustments and improvements in good time. Nevertheless, we must not allow a complete unraveling of policies just because a new leadership takes office, nor must we permit a separate agenda with empty fancy slogans flying all over the place just to show so-called achievements.

(2) We should evaluate the performance of civil servants within a framework that holds them accountable for the goals set for their tenures. It makes no sense that these people can only be promoted and not demoted. It makes little sense, either, that people can be both promoted and demoted. Of course, there should be both promotions and demotions, but only competent officials should be promoted and incompetent ones demoted — no exception should be made in this regard.

(3) Our officials should have a clear understanding of job performance, thinking more about working to lay a solid foundation which is conducive to long-term development and less about competing pointlessly with others, still less about building wasteful, showcase projects to prop up their own image. Let our officials be true and practical, dedicated to work and bold to shoulder their responsibilities, so as to live up to the expectations of history and the people.

(4) The founding of the PRC on October 1, 1949, allowed the Chinese people to stand upright and become the true masters of the country. To change the backward situation starting from scratch, the CPC united and led the people to rely on themselves and strived to build their

homeland with strong determination and concerted effort.

(5) Training in practical circumstances is not a way to get "gilded", nor is it a routine process before promotion. If this is the case, officials will not devote themselves wholeheartedly to the training and will not keep in close touch with the people. The training will only be a show.

(6) We must remain firm in our conviction in Marxism and socialism with Chinese characteristics and strengthen our confidence in the path, theory, system, and culture of socialism with Chinese characteristics. With a stronger sense of historical responsibility and creativity, we should make greater contributions to the development of Marxism. We should never act blindly without assessing how conditions have evolved or allow ourselves to become ossified or closed off, nor should we mechanically imitate others or indiscriminately absorb foreign ideas.

(7) In international affairs, China determines its position and policy based on the fundamental interests of the people both in China and around the world, and on the merits of the issue. China never subordinates itself to others or coerces others into submission. China never provokes trouble, but is not afraid of provocation. Even in a complex and challenging international situation, and faced with external pressure and bullying, China never flinches or bends its knees. We always think on our own, follow our own path and keep our destiny in our own hands.

(8) Already full grown, it was sleek and fat, and its readiness to accept amazed me. It would eat whatever food it came across, sleep wherever there was a place to curl up, waggle its tail and play up to whoever came along, and attach itself to whoever provided its saucer of milk. As a result, unlike my stubborn, intractable sparrow, it survived. Since that time I have detested monsters like that cat who would do anything just to stay alive. To me they are nothing more than a bunch of depraved opportunists, like many more of different types that I have encountered since I have grown up.

(9) I know, as old acquaintances, we've never had to do this for those trivial dealings between us, a gentlemen's agreement was always enough. But, on this deal I'm staking my last penny. Just in case anything should go wrong, however small that possibility may be, let us put our agreement down in black and white. Business is business even between brothers. To ensure that a deal is carried out in a gentlemanly manner, the two parties must have the terms clearly specified at the outset. Later on, the goods can be delivered and payment made accordingly to the satisfaction of both. What d'you think?

3. 段落翻译

ICH (intangible cultural heritage) has become alive and popular across the country as more creative and innovative approaches have been adopted to renew and develop traditional culture. In many places, ICH has found its way into classrooms, as well as into tourist destinations and shopping malls. In poorer counties that are supported by the national government, the Ministry of Culture and Tourism has set up traditional artisanal workshops that hire local people, and thus help bring them more income, as an effective way to eliminate poverty and improve livelihood. In other places, ICH preservation has been included in village rules and regulations, as part of the effort to build a more beautiful countryside. As more traditional art forms and artistry are discovered and developed, and people come to know and love them, ICH will have the vibrancy that allows it to sustain and flourish. Clearly, ICH can promote economic and social progress and benefit us as it becomes part of our life, for us to see and cherish.

第四章　省略与增补

1. 译文补充

(1) the most active and vital force in society; The hopes of a country and the future of a nation lie in the hands of its young generation; have always played a vanguard role in the quest for national rejuvenation

(2) Around the May Fourth Movement in 1919; aspiring and progressive young intellectuals; careful consideration

(3) confident, aspirant and responsible; With a global vision, they stand at the forefront of the times bursting with commitment; a firm belief in Marxism, communism and socialism with Chinese characteristics; sharing weal and woe with the country and the people; being the first in the country to worry about the affairs of the state and the last to enjoy themselves; pioneers in, pacesetters for and contributors to the country's development

(4) the Chinese youth movement would have achieved little; the most valuable experience; the revolutionary traditions passed down are the most precious wealth accumulated over the past century

(5) is a dream about history, the present and the future; cherished by all of the people, but even more so by the young; keep on striving with boundless energy

2. 句子翻译

(1) Beijing has launched five initiatives as part of the country's efforts to pursue a new development approach: building Beijing into a global center for innovation; developing the "two

zones"; growing the digital economy; creating and stimulating demand through supply-side structural reform, and advancing coordinated development between Beijing, Tianjin and Hebei by relocating functions non-essential to Beijing's role as the capital city.

(2) We should stand against drawing lines on ideological grounds, and we should work together to expand common ground and convergence of interests to promote world peace and development.

(3) He who exercises government by means of his virtue may be compared to the north polar star, which keeps its place and all the stars turn towards it.

(4) As the saying goes, "It is more helpful to teach people how to fish than to just give them fish." China will actively implement the "African Talent Program," train 30,000 African professionals in various areas, provide 18,000 government scholarships to Africa between 2013 and 2015, and increase technology transfer and experience sharing with Africa.

(5) This country is its people; the people are the country. As the Communist Party of China has led the people in fighting to establish and develop the People's Republic, it has really been fighting for their support.

(6) After the Ebola epidemic raged through Africa in March, 2014, certain countries closed their embassies and evacuated diplomats and citizens from three West African countries hit by the epidemic. By sharp contrast, the Chinese government helped Africa at the earliest time possible. We sent not only urgently needed supplies but also medical teams of over 1,000 military and civilian doctors to areas stricken most severely by the epidemic. Chinese diplomats and medical experts chose to stay there instead of withdrawing. They fought together with local people until the virus was defeated.

(7) We worked actively to develop the cultural sector. Progress was made in developing major cultural initiatives designed to benefit the public. Great efforts were made to extend radio and television coverage not only to all villages but to all rural homes.

(8) The Song Dynasty statesman Wang Anshi once wrote, "When the law of the land under heaven is good, there will be order in the land under heaven; when the laws of the state are good, there will be order in the state." Following this spirit, we need to ensure that legislation precedes reform. We must place equal emphasis on making new laws, revising existing ones, abolishing those that are outdated, and interpreting laws that need clarification. We must work harder to improve laws, administrative regulations, and local regulations; and further refine a framework of social norms including codes of conduct for citizens, industry rules and regulations, and charters of organizations. This will enable us to lay down the basic foundations for advancing the rule of law.

3. 段落翻译

British philosopher Bertrand Russell once applauded, "... something of the ethical qualities in which China is supreme, and which the modern world most desperately needs." The ideas, humanism, and moral norms embedded in quintessential traditional Chinese culture have not only nourished the spiritual life of the Chinese people and propped up the spiritual world of the whole nation, but also have had a significant value in addressing the common problems confronting humanity. Elemental Chinese culture has constantly nurtured many ethical qualities. From the development concepts of "Tao following the law of nature" and "heaven and man being united as one," to the global ideals of "all nations coexisting in harmony" and "seeking mutual trust and amity with all nations," and finally to the awareness that a community with a shared future should "pull together in times of trouble" and "share weal and woe," these ideas and values have resonated with people around the world. In doing so, they are providing new possibilities for solving the problems facing all mankind. These are the underlying reasons for the growing popularity of the Spring Festival culture around the planet.

第五章　移植与改写

1. 译文补充

(1) way of life; Having a bowl of Laba porridge on the eighth day of the last or the twelfth Chinese lunar month; The Spring Festival is around the corner soon after Laba; bestow auspicious blessings to others in return for good luck; Pottering around a temple fair

(2) pasting spring couplets onto door frames and paper-cuts for window decoration, setting off firecrackers, enjoying reunion dinners, staying up to drink alcohol, visiting kith and kin and presenting them with an artistically written Chinese character "福" (fú, fortune)

(3) On New Year's Eve, we bid a fond farewell to the Old and give a warm welcome to the New

2. 句子翻译

(1) We will not only make the "pie" of social wealth bigger by developing the economy, but also distribute it well on the basis of a rational income distribution system.

(2) Reform and opening up is crucial for driving development.

(3) The imperial court posted a proclamation, inviting any man who could cure him to come

forward. Heaven was touched and sent the Great star of white Gold in the guise of an old man. Announcing he could cure the prince's weeping, the old man took down the proclamation.

(4) In late autumn, during the eighth lunar month, vast stretches of red sorghum shimmered like a sea of blood. Tall and dense, it reeked of glory; cold and graceful, it promised enchantment; passionate and loving, it was tumultuous.

(5) Environmental pollution is a blight on people's quality of life and a trouble that weighs on their hearts. We must fight it with all our might.

(6) Some of his works are thick and heavy in color; some are impressionistic with a dominant green. The slender strokes are even and smooth, and the bold strokes deft and forceful. The charm of nature finds vivid expression through his painting brush.

(7) The "watchdog" let out yelp, leaped a good twenty centimeters into the air, and roared, "You little bastard, who the hell do you think you're talking to? You're dead meat!"

3. 诗歌翻译

Taking Leave of a Friend

Li Bai

Translated by Erza Pound

Blue mountains to the north of the walls,

White river winding about them;

Here we must make separation

And go out through a thousand miles of dead grass.

Mind like a floating wide cloud,

Sunset like the parting of old acquaintances

Who bow over their clasped hands at a distance.

Our horses neigh to each other

As we are departing.

参考文献

［1］巴金.家［M］.北京：人民文学出版社,1953.

［2］曹文轩.青铜葵花［M］.北京：人民文学出版社,天天出版社,2011.

［3］曹雪芹.红楼梦（3版）［M］.北京：人民文学出版社,2008.

［4］陈染.私人生活［M］.南昌：百花洲文艺出版社,2015.

［5］成仿吾.论译诗［J］.中国翻译,1984,（8）：3-6.

［6］程镇球.翻译问题探索：毛选英译研究［M］.北京：商务印书馆,1980.

［7］邓小平.邓小平文选（第一卷）（2版）［M］.北京：人民出版社,1994.

［8］邓小平.邓小平文选（第二卷）（2版）［M］.北京：人民出版社,1994.

［9］邓小平.邓小平文选（第三卷）［M］.北京：人民出版社,1993.

［10］方梦之.翻译策略的理据、要素与特征［J］.上海翻译,2013,（2）：1-6.

［11］方梦之.中外翻译策略类聚——直译、意译、零翻译三元策略框架图［J］.上海翻译,2018,（1）：1-5,95.

［12］冯骥才.三寸金莲［M］.成都：四川文艺出版社,2017.

［13］霍达.穆斯林的葬礼［M］.北京：北京十月文艺出版社,2019.

［14］姜戎.狼图腾［M］.武汉：长江文艺出版社,2004.

［15］杰里米·芒迪.翻译研究入门：理论与应用［M］.上海：上海外语教育出版社,2010.

［16］孔子.论语：The Confucian Analects［M］.Legge J,译.郑州：中州古籍出版社,2016.

［17］李学平.通过翻译学英语［M］.天津：南开大学出版社,2006.

［18］李照国.黄帝内经·素问［M］.西安：世界图书出版公司,2005.

［19］厉以宁.中国经济改革发展之路［M］.凌原,译.北京：外语教学与研究出版社,2013.

［20］连淑能.英汉对比研究［M］.北京：高等教育出版社,1993.

［21］刘重德.文学翻译十讲［M］.北京：中国对外翻译出版公司,1991.

［22］刘宓庆.当代翻译理论［M］.北京：中国对外翻译出版公司,1999.

［23］刘宓庆.新编当代翻译理论［M］.北京：中译出版社,2019.

［24］刘宓庆.论翻译的虚实观［J］.中国翻译,1984（10）：14-17.

［25］刘宓庆.翻译美学导论［M］.北京：中译出版社,2019.

［26］刘震云.一地鸡毛［M］.武汉：长江文艺出版社,2004.

［27］刘震云.一句顶一万句［M］.武汉：长江文艺出版社,2009.

［28］鲁迅.阿Q正传（插图本）［M］.杨宪益,戴乃迭,译.北京：新世界出版社,2000.

［29］罗贯中.三国演义［M］.北京：人民文学出版社,1998.

［30］毛泽东.毛泽东选集［M］.北京：人民出版社,1991.

［31］莫言.红高粱家族［M］.北京：当代世界出版社,2004.

［32］莫言.檀香刑［M］.北京：作家出版社,2001.

［33］庞焱.可译性和不可译性——以日汉互译为例［J］.外语研究,2009（2）：87-88.

［34］钱锺书.围城［M］.珍妮·凯利,茅国权,译.北京：人民出版社,2003.

［35］琼-平卡姆.中式英语之鉴［M］.北京：外语教学与研究出版社,2000.

［36］乔萍,瞿淑蓉,宋洪玮.散文佳作108篇［M］.南京：译林出版社,2002.

［37］沈从文.边城［M］.北京：北京十月文艺出版社,2008.

［38］施耐庵,罗贯中.水浒传［M］.北京：人民文学出版社,2021.

［39］苏童.河岸［M］.北京：人民文学出版社,2009.

［40］苏童.碧奴：孟姜女哭长城的传说［M］.重庆：重庆出版社,2006.

［41］唐圭璋.全宋词［M］.北京：中华书局,1965.

［42］吴承恩.西游记［M］.北京：人民文学出版社,2010.

［43］习近平.摆脱贫困［M］.福州：福建人民出版社,1992.

［44］习近平.习近平二十国集团领导人杭州峰会讲话选编［M］.北京：外文出版社,2017.

［45］习近平.习近平金砖国家领导人厦门会晤重要讲话［M］.北京：外文出版社,2018.

［46］习近平.习近平谈治国理政（第一卷）［M］.北京：外文出版社,2014.

［47］习近平.习近平谈治国理政（第二卷）［M］.北京：外文出版社,2017.

［48］习近平.习近平谈治国理政（第三卷）［M］.北京：外文出版社,2020.

［49］熊兵.翻译研究中的概念混淆——以"翻译策略""翻译方法"和"翻译技巧"为例［J］.中国翻译,2014,35（3）：82-88.

［50］杨红樱.淘气包马小跳：四个调皮蛋［M］.南宁：接力出版社,2003.

［51］杨绛.失败的经验（试谈翻译）［J］.中国翻译,1986,（5）：23-29.

［52］叶子南.基本功还是灵活与变通［J］.中国翻译,2019,40（5）：176-178.

［53］余华.许三观卖血记［M］.海口：南海出版公司,1998.

［54］余华.在细雨中呼喊［M］.北京：作家出版社,2012.

［55］郁达夫.春风沉醉的晚上［M］.长沙：新世纪出版社,1998.

［56］曾剑平.汉英翻译的虚实转换［J］.中国科技翻译,2006,（1）：9-11,18.

［57］张景,张松辉.道德经［M］.北京：中华书局,2021.

［58］张培基.英译中国现代散文选（第二辑）［M］.上海：上海外语教育出版社,2003.

［59］张燕婴.论语［M］.北京：中华书局,2006.

［60］赵树理.小二黑结婚［M］.北京：文化发展出版社,2021.

［61］中国外文出版发行事业局,当代中国与世界研究院,中国翻译研究院.中国关键词：生态文明篇（汉英对照）［M］.北京：新世界出版社,2022.

［62］中国人民银行.中国人民银行2019年度报告［R/OL］.［2022-12-02］.http://www.pbc. gov.cn/chubanwu/114566/115296/4106701/4106565/20200930164452471804.pdf.

［63］中华人民共和国国务院台湾事务办公室,中华人民共和国国务院新闻办公室.台湾问 题与新时代中国统一事业［R/OL］.(2022-08-10)［2022-12-02］.http://www.scio.gov. cn/zfbps/zfbps_2279/202209/t20220916_330283.html.

［64］中华人民共和国国务院新闻办公室.2021中国的航天［R/OL］.(2022-01-28)［2022- 12-02］.http://www.scio.gov.cn/zfbps/zfbps_2279/202207/t20220704_130725.html.

［65］中华人民共和国国务院新闻办公室.新时代的中国青年［R/OL］.(2022-04-21) ［2022-12-02］.http://www.scio.gov.cn/zfbps/zfbps_2279/202207/t20220704_130735.html.

［66］中华人民共和国国务院新闻办公室.中国的生物多样性保护［R/OL］.(2021-10-08) ［2022-12-02］.http://www.scio.gov.cn/ztk/dtzt/44689/47139/index.htm.

［67］中华人民共和国国务院新闻办公室.中国应对气候变化的政策与行动［R/OL］. (2021-10-27)［2022-12-02］.http://www.scio.gov.cn/ztk/dtzt/44689/47315/index.htm.

［68］钟述孔.英汉翻译手册［M］.北京：世界知识出版社,1997.

［69］朱虹,周欣.嬉雪：中国当代女性散文选(汉英对照本)［M］.沈阳：辽宁教育出版社, 2002.

［70］Candlin C M. The Herald Wind: Translations of Sung Dynasty Poems, Lyrics and Songs. London: John Murray, 1933.

［71］Cao Xueqin, Gao E. A Dream of Red Mansions. Yang Xianyi, Yang G, Trans. Beijing: Foreign Languages Press, 1978-1980.

［72］Cao Xueqin, Gao E. The Story of the Stone (Volume I-V). Hawkes D, Minford J, Trans. Harmondsworth: Penguin, 1973-1986.

［73］Cao Wenxuan. Bronze and Sunflower. Wang H, Trans. London: Candlewick Press, 2017.

［74］Capan Z G, dos Reis F, Grasten M. The Politics of Translation in International Relations. London: Palgrave Macmillan, 2021.

［75］Catford J C. A Linguistic Theory of Translation: An Essay in Applied Linguistics. Oxford: Oxford University Press, 1965.

［76］Chen Ran. A Private Life. Howard-Gibbon J, Trans. New York, NY: Columbia University Press, 2004.

［77］Deng Xiaoping. Selected Works of Deng Xiaoping (Volume I-III). Beijing: Foreign Languages Press, 1984-1994.

［78］Feng Jicai. The Three-Inch Golden Lotus: A Novel on Foot Binding. Wakefield D, Trans. Honolulu, HI: University of Hawaii Press, 1994.

［79］Huo Da. The Jade King: History of a Chinese Muslim Family. Guan Yuehua, Zhong

Liangbi, Trans. Beijing: Foreign Languages Press, 1992.

［80］ Jiang Rong. Wolf Totem. Goldblatt H, Trans. New York, NY: Penguin Books, 2008.

［81］ Koller W. Einführung in die Übersetzungswissenschaft ([Research into the Science of Translation]). Heidelberg: Quelle & Meyer, 1979.

［82］ Landau, J. Beyond Spring: Tz'u Poems of the Sung Dynasty. New York, NY: Columbia University Press, 1997.

［83］ Lao Tzu. Tao Te Ching. Waley A, Trans. London: Wordsworth Editions Ltd, 1999.

［84］ Lefevere A. Translation, Rewriting, and the Manipulation of Literary Fame. London: Routledge, 1992.

［85］ Liu Zhenyun. Ground Covered with Chicken Feathers. Kwan D, Trans. Beijing: Foreign Languages Teaching and Research Press, 2014.

［86］ Liu Zhenyun. Someone to Talk to. Goldblatt H, Lin S L, Trans. Durham, NC: Duke University Press, 2018.

［87］ Lo Kuan-chung. Romance of the Three Kingdoms. Brewitt-Taylor C H, Trans. Singapore: Tuttle Publishing, 2002.

［88］ Luo Guanzhong. Three Kingdoms: A Historical Novel. Roberts M, Trans. Berkeley, CA: University of California Press, 1991.

［89］ Mao Zedong. Selected Works of Mao Tse-Tung (Volume I-V). Beijing: Foreign Languages Press, 1964−1977.

［90］ Mo Yan. Red Sorghum. Goldblatt H, Trans. New York, NY: Penguin Books, 1994.

［91］ Mo Yan. Sandalwood Death: A Novel. Goldblatt H, Trans. Norman, OK: University of Oklahoma Press, 2013.

［92］ Newmark P. Approaches to Translation. London: Prentice Hall, 1988.

［93］ Ni Maoshing. The Yellow Emperor's Classic of Medicine: A New Translation of the Neijing Suwen with Commentary. Boulder, CO: Shambhala, 1995.

［94］ Pa Chin. The Family. Shapiro S, Trans. Beijing: Foreign Languages Press, 1978.

［95］ Qian Zhongshu. Fortress Besieged. Kelly J, Mao N K, Trans. London: Penguin, 2004.

［96］ Sallis J. On Translation. Bloomington, IN: Indiana University Press, 2002.

［97］ Shen Congwen. Border Town. Kinkley J C, Trans. New York, NY: Harper Perennial, 2009.

［98］ Shi Nai'an, Luo Guanzhong. The Marshes of Mount Liang (Part 1−5). Dent-Young J, Dent-Young A, Trans. Hong Kong: Chinese University Press, 1994−2002.

［99］ Shi Nai'an. The Water Margin: Outlaws of the Marsh. Jackson J H, Trans. North Clarendon, VT: Tuttle Publishing, 2010.

［100］ Shi Nai'an, Luo Guanzhong. Outlaws of the Marsh. Shapiro S, Trans. Beijing: Foreign

Languages Press, 1980.

[101] Strunk W. The Elements of Style. London: Macmillan, 1972.

[102] Su Tong. Binu and the Great Wall. Goldblatt H, Trans. Edinburgh: Canongate, 2007.

[103] Su Tong. The Boat to Redemption. Goldblatt H, Trans. London: Doubleday, 2010.

[104] The People's Bank of China. The People's Bank of China 2019 Annual Report [R/OL]. [2022−12−02]. http://www.pbc.gov.cn/en/3688110/3688259/3689032/3709448/3984236/4188833/2021020518200911862.pdf.

[105] The State Council Information Office of the People's Republic of China. *Biodiversity Conservation in China* [R/OL]. (2021−10−08) [2022−12−02]. http://www.scio.gov.cn/ztk/dtzt/44689/47139/index.htm.

[106] The State Council Information Office of the People's Republic of China. China's Space Program: A 2021 Perspective. (2022−01−28) [2022−12−02]. http://www.scio.gov.cn/ztk/dtzt/47678/47826/47834/Document/1719715/1719715.htm.

[107] The State Council Information Office of the People's Republic of China. Responding to Climate Change: China's Policies and Actions. (2021−10−27) [2022−12−02]. http://www.scio.gov.cn/ztk/dtzt/44689/47315/index.htm.

[108] The State Council Information Office of the People's Republic of China. Youth of China in the New Era. (2022−08−10) [2022−12−02]. http://www.scio.gov.cn/zfbps/ndhf/2022n/202304/t20230407_710480.html.

[109] The Taiwan Affairs Office of the State Council of the People's Republic of China, the State Council Information Office of the People's Republic of China. The Taiwan Question and China's Reunification in the New Era. (2022−08−10) [2022−12−02]. http://www.scio.gov.cn/zfbps/ndhf/2022n/202304/t20230407_710482.html.

[110] Unschuld P U, Hermann T. Huang Di Nei Jing Su Wen: Annotated Translation of Huang Di's Inner Classic — Basic Questions. Berkeley, CA: University of California Press, 2011.

[111] van Doorslaser L. Risking Conceptual Maps: Mapping as a Keywords-related Tool Underlying the Online *Translation Studies Bibliography*//Gambier Y, van Doorslaser L. The Metalanguage of Translation. Amsterdam: John Benjamins, 2009: 27−43.

[112] Veith I. Huang Ti Nei Ching Su Wen: The Yellow Emperor's Classic of Internal Medicine. Berkeley, CA: University of California Press, 1970.

[113] Wu Cheng'en. Monkey. Waley A, Trans. London: Penguin Classics, 1994.

[114] Wu Cheng'en. Monkey King: Journey to the West. Lovell J, Trans. London: Penguin Classics, 2021.

［115］Wu Cheng'en. The Journey to the West (Revised Edition). Yu A C, Trans. Chicago, IL: University Of Chicago Press, 2012.

［116］Xi Jinping. The Governance of China I. Beijing: Foreign Languages Press, 2014.

［117］Xi Jinping. The Governance of China II. Beijing: Foreign Languages Press, 2017.

［118］Xi Jinping. The Governance of China III. Beijing: Foreign Languages Press, 2020.

［119］Xi Jinping. Up and Out of Poverty. Beijing: Foreign Languages Press, 2016.

［120］Yu Hua. Chronicle of a Blood Merchant. Jones A F, Trans. New York: Pantheon Books, 2003.

［121］Yu Hua. Cries in the Drizzle. Barr A H, Trans. New York, NY: Anchor, 2008.

［122］Yang Hongying. Mo's Mischief: Four Troublemakers. London: HarperCollins Publishers, 2008.

［123］Yu Dafu. Nights of Spring Fever and Other Writings. Beijing: Chinese Literature Press, 1984.